PSI SUCCESSFUL BUSINESS LIBRARY

D0520305

Managing People

A Practical Guide

by Byron Lane and
Richard Rierdan

The Oasis Press®/PSI Research
Central Point, Oregon

Published by The Oasis Press®
© 1985, 1990, 1996, 2001 by Byron Lane

This publication is designed to provide accurate and authoritative information in regard to the subject matter covered. It is sold with the understanding that the publisher is not engaged in rendering legal, accounting, or other professional service. If legal advice or other expert assistance is required, the services of a competent professional person should be sought.
— from a declaration of principles jointly adopted by a committee of the American Bar Association and a committee of publishers.

Managing Editor and Book Designer: Constance C. Dickinson
Assistant Editor: Gina Froelich
Typographer: Jan Olsson
Cover Designer: J. C. Young

Please direct any comments, questions, or suggestions regarding this book to
The Oasis Press®/ PSI Research:

    Editorial Department
    P.O. Box 3727
    Central Point, OR 97502
    (541) 245-6502
    info@psi-research.com *e-mail*

The Oasis Press® is a Registered Trademark of Publishing Services, Inc.,
an Oregon corporation doing business as PSI Research.

Library of Congress Cataloging-in-Publication Data

Lane, Byron.
    Managing people : a practical guide / Byron Lane, Richard Rierdan.-- 4th ed.
      p. cm. -- (The PSI successful business library)
    Includes index.
    ISBN 1-55571-554-0
    1. Personnel management--Handbooks, manuals, etc. 2. Personnel
management--United States--Handbooks, manuals, etc. 3. Career
development--Handbooks, manuals, etc. I. Rierdan, Richard. II. Title. III. Series.
HF5549.17.L36 2001
658.3--dc21   2001034360

Printed in the United States of America
Fourth edition 10 9 8 7 6 5 4 3 2 1

 Printed on recycled paper when available.

Table of Contents

To Donald R. Sime, our Founding Dean and mentor.
Your inspiration, support and friendship has made this possible

Preface

Everyone arrives at a management position or at business ownership with a substantial amount of technical skill. It's unthinkable that anyone would be in a leadership position without a solid understanding of the major components of the job he or she is doing. Yet many people who become managers lack even rudimentary people skills.

In management, the ability to work with people becomes increasingly more important the higher you go, while technical knowledge becomes less important. First-line supervisors spend approximately twenty percent of their time managing and eighty percent doing. Middle to senior managers should be spending more than fifty percent of their time managing. Small business owners or senior executives are managing almost ninety percent of the time and doing direct work only ten percent. The managing portion always involves people.

The assumption that a good technical person or one with good general business knowledge makes a good manager is simply not true. The essential skill of management is the ability to develop and work with people.

The problem for most managers is compounded by the fact that their technical expertise leads them to see people as objects or units of production. Computer or engineering knowledge bears no relationship to people knowledge. Moving from product orientation to people orientation requires a complete shift of the psyche. Clearly, a rigid product orientation, no matter how expert, is not enough. However, every manager willing to try new behaviors and new ways of viewing the world can acquire people skills.

This book is designed to take you beyond the thinking process, to help you develop sensing, feeling, and intuiting skills. In some cases, this means taking risks: discussing issues you never talked about before; communicating in new ways; considering new views of people; making changes in the way you believe, in the way you behave, and in the way you manage.

This is a real challenge. Most managers are successful in making the transition because they find their new people skills personally rewarding — even the learning process is exciting.

You will recognize that you have been successful when the people in your organization have better interpersonal relationships, reduced stress, improved health, lower absenteeism and turnover — all adding up to improved productivity.

An additional byproduct of becoming a better manager of people is personal growth for you! You will find yourself enjoying your work more, feeling better physically, having a higher energy level, finding new rewards in your personal life. Unbelievable, you say? Try it and see!

Acknowledgments

The students in our MBA classes in the Graziadio School of Business and Management at Pepperdine University provided their workplace experiences which became all the case studies we will ever need. Their willingness to apply the concepts from this book really tested what otherwise might just be words.

Much of the substance of Chapter 10, Understanding Culture, is owed to the work of Dr. Len Korot. Dr. Ed Rockey provided material for Chapter 1, Thinking Strategically. Many thanks to Dr. Phyllis Herrin, a consultant on workforce diversity, who did the editing to make our language non-gender specific. Judith Simpson contributed invaluable writing on her specialty, dialogue, an important part of the first chapter. Ida Fisher-Lane was proof reader and inspiration provider.

Chapter 1

Test Yourself on Strategic Thinking

Being an effective manager and developer of people requires the ability to think strategically. Answer the questions, then turn to the end of the chapter to see how you rate.

	Yes	No
1. I base my decisions on facts.	☐	☐
2. I am a thoughtful person with both feet on the ground.	☐	☐
3. I solve problems by looking for patterns and going with hunches.	☐	☐
4. I mostly rely on images in thinking and remembering.	☐	☐
5. I prefer formal lectures to group discussions.	☐	☐
6. I like open-ended questions.	☐	☐
7. I am essentially an emotional person.	☐	☐
8. I am rational and reliable.	☐	☐
9. I like being fluid and spontaneous.	☐	☐
10. I need to control my feelings.	☐	☐

Chapter 1

Thinking Strategically

Defining the Art of Strategic Thinking

As business becomes increasingly global and more complex, conventional ways of thinking, analyzing data, solving problems, making decisions, and responding to change are inadequate, even obsolete.

Fewer situations are cut-and-dried, and unfamiliar conditions require the ability to think at new levels. To do this, the new leaders must learn the art of strategic thinking through a shift of mind, from seeing parts to seeing wholes, from reacting to the present to creating the future. They must learn to see interrelationships rather than linear cause/effect sequences, and see all change as a continual process rather than as a series of snapshots of isolated events.

A prime example of linear versus strategic thinking occurred when many United States management teams got caught in the core dilemma, as they saw it, of having to choose between low cost or high quality. Many chose low cost and the few that chose high quality saw themselves aiming at a high-quality, high-price market niche. Seeing the answer as an either/or choice has turned out disastrous for some United States manufacturers as foreign firms have chosen consistently to improve both quality and cost.

In the past, strategic thinking was left to top-level executives whose jobs were to manage the whole company. Today mid-level managers are involved in team decisions and make input to long-range planning, both of which require strategic thinking. More to the point of this book, managing human resources defies the common linear-thinking process, but instead requires the ability to deal with people in the context of their whole lives, rather than seeing them as units of production.

The problem begins in our schools, where almost every facet of our educational system is based on valuing the right answer, of knowing the facts. Providing the correct answer is how we measure a student's progress. This pattern continues in business. Such a rigid, analytic, step-by-step approach to problem-solving favors words, numbers, and facts presented in logical sequence. Such logical sequencing leads to crisis management, prevalent in much of the business world, but particularly in small businesses where many decisions are made reactively with little thought to the long term. A more creative approach would prefer insight, images, concepts, and patterns — all synthesized into an intuitive whole. The latter approach leads to seeing the organization in its larger context and may be better suited to a rapidly changing environment.

Business schools are not much help in breaking out of the linear-thinking mode. Most management education is tilted towards logic and, because of its content and orientation, attracts people who are dominant in that way. In effect, it preaches to believers. The result is a vast array of business school graduates whose training enables them to function only at the operational end of the business, rather than giving them the potential for leadership that requires strategizing with its emphasis on vision, insight, inference, intuition, trends, patterns, integration, synthesis, projections, risk, and global thinking.

A young executive in our class in Human Resources Management had just received a promotion and his company was putting him through the strategically-oriented MBA program. He readily grasped the concepts, was a good oral communicator, and was rapidly putting into practice in his own organization the new ideas he was learning. But whenever he was asked to write about his reading and his experiences, or to put together his ideas in a comprehensive way, he failed miserably. During one-on-one conversations it was learned that, prior to going into business, he had been a musician, leading a band and writing published songs.

One day on a hunch, we asked him to write his next paper in music, to put his thoughts into a song. What evolved was a wonderful, musical journey into the realm of people in organizations. Why did music allow him to express himself so beautifully when he failed so completely in prose? As is so common throughout the United States, his education had been oriented to linear, logical processes. He had learned to write in a way that would elicit commendations for his ability to organize, but that left the content empty of value. When asked to try music, he was freed to switch to his creative mode where he could deal with the material in a holistic way. The results were astounding and a clear example of how demand for "logic" puts a severe damper on the most creative talent.

A Dutch fairy tale tells of the young boy who, while walking along the dike, sees a trickle of water coming through. He knows that if he does nothing, the water will enlarge the hole and the dike will collapse, flooding the country. He puts his thumb in the hole, stops the water, and saves Holland. The current equivalents are engineering managers who, informed of an equipment failure, rush out to the factory floor, take off their coats, roll up their sleeves, and fix the problem.

The Dutch story is a lovely one, and the description of managers invariably elicits admiration for their skills. In a contemporary organizational context, however, these are illustrations of a terrible management style. Had our engineers been managers who employed strategic thinking, they would have embraced a "developer" style and would have set up training sessions, enabling each member of their teams to repair the equipment. They could have devoted their attention to leadership, the real essence of management.

Strategic Thinking as Systems Thinking

A giant step in the direction of strategic thinking is to begin seeing the relationships in the whole system rather than looking at things as a sum of the parts. If you take a system apart to identify its components, and then operate these components in such a way that each behaves as well as it can, you can be almost certain that the *system* will not behave as well as it can. This is because fine-tuning the parts does not assure that the parts will work well together in the entire system.

If you could get a hundred of the world's best automobiles together and you took the best transmission from one, the best carburetor from another, the best distributor you could find, until you had all the parts to assemble a car, then you ought to have the best one possible. But you won't get an auto mobile if the parts don't fit together into a cohesive whole.

Performance does not have to do with the quality of the individual parts alone but is a consequence of the relationship between the performance of the parts. Similarly, when you work on upgrading the performance of the departments of a business and get each operating as efficiently as you can, the business as a whole may not be operating efficiently.

In any organization (system) the performance as a whole is affected by every one of the parts. The way any part can relate to the whole depends on what other parts are doing. For example: marketing may want to increase sales by lowering a price, but is dependent on what production can do to reduce costs.

It has been our experience that many executives see themselves as superior problem solvers, and that is often true when the decision has little to do with the overall performance of the organization. Yet we've observed seasoned executives, who fully understand the important effect people in the organization have on corporate results, totally ignore this factor when deciding on strategic options. The impact of the human side of the organization has the same effect on strategic outcomes as finance, manufacturing, or any other part of the company.

When you become a real strategic thinker, the benefits of teamwork and collaboration, as covered in chapters 2 and 3, become readily apparent. Acquiring the ability to think strategically is essential to becoming an effective leader of people, one who integrates the human side of the enterprise into the overall planning and operation of the company.

Integrative Management

Change-resistant organizations are usually dominated by logical thinkers and display cultures that are impervious to any attempt to introduce integrative techniques. By not honoring strategic thinkers, they become increasingly incapable of innovative operation — a sure path to failure in our global environment. A compelling reason to foster strategic thinking is that it offers the only way to deal effectively with change. This is not to say that business should de-emphasize the logical style, but rather that the two styles should be applied where appropriate.

Many women are joining the ranks of corporate management and many are leaving to start their own businesses. Their success in both situations is well documented and easily understood. Women bring to their leadership roles an enhanced capability, the result of differing enculturation. On average, women are more intuitive, more open to new ideas, and more people oriented. This is quite apparent in our MBA classes where women readily accept and apply the human resources management principles advocated throughout this book. They quickly become proficient at strategic-planning processes. Although this gives female executives an advantage in the near term, changes in our culture are making it more acceptable for men in management to develop and incorporate these people-oriented skills in their style, promising an equalization of strategic abilities over time.

For any organization striving to make its workplace creative and innovative, the greatest need is learning how to manage differences. A manager whose mental preference is limited to the linear style often finds it hard to accept the mental preference of employees who have radically different ways of thinking. Such managers are more comfortable with homogeneity and typically lack the ability to lead a heterogeneous team. While learning to manage differences isn't easy, it is less complicated for the manager with an integrated linear and strategic approach.

Characteristics of the Strategic Thinker

The leader or manager who aspires to superior performance would do well to consider some of the recognizable characteristics of the strategic thinker.

- Innovative thinkers avoid symptomatic solutions; they think of larger issues and the longer term.

- They don't argue about what is real. They know that the only reality is perception, which varies with each person.

- They eschew the practice of breaking things into components for study; instead they look for relationships between the components.

- Allowing their belief systems to be challenged is always acceptable; they know that a rigidly held belief system is not open to new input.

- Far beyond simple problem-solving, visionary leaders anticipate the future, setting high goals and inspiring others to achieve them.

- Strategic thinkers know that their world views are sets of assumptions rather than facts, and that all assumptions are open to inquiry.

- Strategic thinkers see how most organizational problems have causes and effects that are distant in time and space and realize solutions often require interventions that are subtle and not always obvious. This is in contrast to linear thinking where the complexity of details is in the foreground and solutions are applied piecemeal.

- Teamwork is important to strategists because it brings together different thinking modes and applies a rounded experience to the problem. While heterogenous teams are more difficult to manage, strategic thinkers find this simply challenging.

- In the traditional organization, leaders are admired as charismatic decision makers. In the new organization model, strategic thinking leaders are designers, teachers, and developers, responsible for building organizations and helping people continually expand their capabilities.

- Strategic thinkers do not expect organizational problems to arise in one place. Every part of the organization is part of the system and everyone shares responsibility for problems that develop.

- Lessons can be learned from Native American leaders who, when making tribal decisions, considered the effect of their choices on the seventh generation yet to come.

Strategies for New Ways of Thinking

Strategic thinking requires the ability to communicate openly. This becomes most apparent in teamwork. While we often assume that great teams avoid conflict, the reality is that conflict is natural and productive. Conflicting ideas are critical for discovering new solutions that would not be arrived at on one's own.

In poorly-led teams, conflict may lead to polarization or indifference. At the bottom of such problems is how we deal with defensiveness. Defensive routines are entrenched habits we use to protect ourselves from the threat we perceive if we expose our thinking. Defensiveness is fostered in organizations where it is perceived as unsafe not to have the answer at all times. While the use of defensive routines may protect us from the pain of the moment, they are anathema to fully productive functioning in the managerial role.

One of the first steps in becoming a master of strategic thinking is to become aware of your own defensive routines. As you use the various materials in this book, you will find many suggestions for opening up, both to yourself and others. For suggestions on how to reduce defensive routines within a team, see the discussion Engaging Your Organization in Dialogue later in this chapter.

Strategic thinking always involves an attempt to see the relationship between each decision you make and its effect on the larger organization. Constantly make connections, and always remember that nothing in management is a stand-alone issue — everything is interconnected. If you are making a human resources decision, examine first what effect it will have on other members of your organization, what spillover might occur into another manager's department, what effect it might have on both immediate and long-range productivity. By constantly attempting to think and visualize in larger wholes you will continue to become a more effective strategic thinker.

Bringing Mind Patterns into Consciousness

The Danish philosopher, Søren Kierkegaard, said a person can be fooled in two ways: one is to believe what isn't so; the other is to refuse to believe what is so. The greatest portion of our total mental activity goes on outside our conscious awareness. Our perceptions, attitudes, values, and behavior are influenced far more by what is going on in unconscious mind patterns than by what is accessible to the conscious mind. Our reality, then, is strongly influenced by unconsciously held beliefs. People who grow up in different cultures perceive different realities. Holding slavishly to one's own perception of reality leads down a narrow path of decision making in a corporate or personal strategy. Becoming aware of one's own belief system and allowing it to be challenged is a major step in the ability to think strategically.

One of our executive students tells this story:

"As a young CEO leading a growing organization, I was hard driving and one-dimensional. Everything I did was operationally oriented so I would manage from one crisis to the next, constantly putting out fires. My whole focus was on winning small battles, and I received many kudos for my outstanding performance from many of my associates who were also short-term oriented.

Only when the business began to experience serious problems was I willing to examine my mind patterns. I discovered that I was playing an unconscious game called "Beat Your Dad." My father had been an extraordinary entrepreneur, very inventive in the field of merchandising, and was beloved by everyone who knew him. My game plan (subconscious, of course) was to be better than him. To achieve this I had to keep showing positive, visible results and have them confirmed by my peers. This myopia caused me to build an organization with an eye on today only and with little thought to the future, a total absence of strategic thinking and planning.

Only when I was willing to bring this mind pattern into everyday consciousness was I able to see that my abilities were different from my father's and laudable in their own right. Then I could let go of the game, refocus on my own competencies, and become effective as a strategic leader."

Moving Toward Strategic Thinking

- Constantly question your model of reality, rethink your world view, and unfreeze your mind patterns so you can examine alternative possibilities in a much larger framework.

- Improve thinking by shifting from mind patterns that are a series of snapshots to mind patterns that perceive longer-term change.

- Discipline yourself to remain aware of the whole and resist the desire to analyze the parts *ad infinitum.*

- Be a perpetual student, finding new ways to learn.

- Learn to see yourself, others, and the world through a global perspective. It is said that a rock thrown into the ocean ripples on a shore thousands of miles away.

- Reality is of your own creation; reframe your basic belief system into something with greater possibility for releasing more of your potential.

- Mind patterns are formed in childhood. Recognizing these patterns gives you the power to change.

Techniques to Enhance Strategic Thinking

Edward Rockey, Ph.D., Professor of Behavioral Science at Pepperdine University's School of Business and Management, teaches a course in creativity for MBA students. The key concepts that follow have been compiled by Dr. Rockey and used both in his own classes and when he is working with Executive MBA students in special sessions examining strategic thinking.

- Create an Affirmation. Repeating a statement that has not yet become a reality tends to increase awareness of and commitment to that statement. Many great inventors and discoverers affirmed their visions before they created or encountered them.

- Construct Alternative Scenarios. Creating "What if ...." plots can prompt the mind to consider possibilities and outcomes that might otherwise be overlooked. Select a problem you are encountering, then create scenarios in your mind, imagining alternative responses.

- Have an Appetite for Chaos. To deal imaginatively with the intricacies of change, do an affirmation, telling yourself that you welcome uncertainty and confusion because it stimulates your imagination.

- Try Mind/Body Disciplines. Yoga, Aikido, Tai Chi, and similar practices heighten awareness and blend with focused activity. Such practices can also suspend "mind chatter," which alone can assist the creative process.

- Explore Brainstorming. Probably the best-known creativity enhancement technique, this method involves the random, nonjudgmental listing of spontaneous ideas. It is often used as a group process.

- Practice Centering. Centering is easier to experience than describe. Some people sense it happening as they concentrate on the physical center of the body, near the navel. Others enhance it when they focus on senses, such as listening to specific sounds. Centering can also be achieved by concentrating on breathing. The mind/body disciplines described above also enhance centering.

- Do Dream Work. Noted mathematicians, inventors, scientists, and other creative professionals have testified to the value of recalling and programming dreams.

- Make Forced Associations. Connect ideas, processes, objects, or situations that seemingly have no connection.

- Take a Fantastic Voyage. Visualize yourself as one element in a process or one particle in an object. Then imagine yourself traveling through the situation or object.

- Generate Wild Ideas. List suggestions spontaneously, no matter how outrageous, how unlikely, how absurd, or how unscientific. Later you can examine them and do a careful analysis.

- Watch a Movie of the Mind. Many inventors, scientists, artists, executives, athletes, and psychologists have testified to the power of visualization and other forms of imagery. Pictures in the mind's eye offer vistas that expand awareness and integrate data.

- Listen to Music. Try anything soothing, but largo music seems to help the creative process most.

- Relax, Take a Break. Get as much factual information as you can, put it in order, test it. Then relax and let it incubate for awhile. An "aha!" often comes when you are off guard.

Blocks to Strategic Thinking

Limits placed on us in school:

- Daydreaming is a waste of time.
- Humor is out of place. Get serious.
- Playfulness is for children.
- Logic and math are good; intuition and feelings are bad.
- Making a mistake is not acceptable.
- Creativity is rare.

Limits we place on ourselves:

- Accept the first plausible answer.
- Overly structure the mind.
- Have a low tolerance for frustration.
- Freeze on limited data.
- Use the same methods over and over.

- Resist change.

- Mistrust intuition.

- Have a low tolerance for ambiguity.

- Stay inflexible.

- Follow tunnel vision.

- Stereotype.

- Be judgmental.

- Consistently think in linear patterns.

Limits placed by organizations:

- That's not the way we do it around here.

- If it ain't broke don't fix it.

- You have our support, but don't get out of line.

- Well, it's tradition.

- Here's where you fit in the organizational box.

- Decisions are made at the top.

- Make a mistake and you're history.

- Don't make waves.

Engaging Your Organization in Dialogue

The material for an understanding of dialogue was prepared by Judith Simpson, Organization Development Consultant, who conducts workshops and training in dialogue for businesses, organizations, and consulting groups. To contact her, see the Additional Information page at the end of this chapter.

When asked to describe the situation where their creative ideas flow, the situation most conducive to thinking strategically, many people say it is when they are in the shower or while driving alone.

Common to both these situations is being safely contained, with full control, in a nonjudgmental environment. While driving requires somewhat more attention than taking a shower, both are everyday activities, done quite automatically, with no one to interrupt the train of thought.

Imagine the possibility of carrying such a personal comfort level into a group setting where you can verbalize your thoughts and learn through the ideas of others, all in an accepting, open, nonthreatening atmosphere where no one chooses a side. This is possible under conditions of dialogue, a group process where members suspend assumptions and judgment for a specific time period, in order to think, speak, and listen together.

Dialogue is characterized by attentive listening and nondefensive speaking, where all ideas are heard and respected so that everyone can learn from them. It can create trust and improve the quality of a self-managed team, a management team, or any work group meeting together to advance productivity. Dialogue can be an ongoing activity in a learning organization or a means to better understanding before beginning a decision-making process. While simple in concept, dialogue requires practice to enhance communication skills. Before engaging in dialogue, everyone must commit to seeking continuous improvement in skills and attitudes, and agree to follow these basic guidelines:

- People sit in a circle so they can see and hear each other face to face. The circle may may be viewed as a container for the ideas. The boundary of the circle can keep out behaviors that restrict thinking. People address everyone in the circle, or may speak to the center of the circle if they wish.

- People agree to set aside their positions and titles for the time limit of the dialogue.

- Dialogue takes place in a set time limit, such as twenty minutes to an hour. Everyone agrees beforehand to honor this limit.

- There is usually a subject decided before the dialogue. A short reading may introduce the subject.

- No one interrupts another. Speakers, knowing they have the time they need to speak, will work to make their ideas clear and to the point.

- Speakers do not have to defend anything they say. They are asked to tell their truth as they see it at the moment. No questions are asked during a dialogue. People can, however, ask someone to clarify or tell how they came to believe what they say, assuming the request represents interest or curiosity, rather than subtle disagreement or a need to play devil's advocate.

- People temporarily set aside judgment. We all judge, but we are capable of suspending judgment for periods of time to simply hear what others think. Since dialogue has no need for outcomes or decisions, there is no need to judge.

- There is no cross talk, no problem-solving. These behaviors can turn into two-way conversations that separate people from the group.

Begin your dialogue session by appointing a facilitator to remind the group of the guidelines and to monitor time. Such a person is a regular member of the group with an added duty.

Dialogue should be a special time set aside for learning and thinking, not for seeking solutions to problems. Once the procedure is well established, however, you can hold a dialogue prior to meetings where consensus is needed to reach a decision. When used this way, dialogue often speeds up the decision-making process.

Entered into with a willingness to follow the guidelines, with open minds and open hearts, dialogue can elevate the process of an entire organization.

Creating Your Personal Strategic Plan

One way to increase your ability to think strategically is to take a holistic look at your own life. The process of creating your own strategic plan will help you to see the relationship among the influences in your past, your behavior in the present, and the possibilities for your future. As you progress through this series of exercises you will gain insights into the nature of strategic thinking. When you are finished you will have a program that can be used to create your life the way you want it to be, and that will be consonant with your ability to achieve your goals.

Work each exercise as a separate unit — do not try to do too much at one time. You will find the introspection challenging and enjoyable. For many, doing this personal strategic plan has created a major breakthrough in their careers.

Self-Image

This exercise is a journey into your past, examining the thoughts, feelings, events, relationships, themes, and dreams that have helped to form who you are now.

Begin by finding a comfortable seat in a darkened room, with no distracting sounds. If you do deep relaxation exercises, go into a fully relaxed state. If you've not worked previously on deep relaxation techniques, simply settle into the chair, or lie down, and let yourself progressively relax each set of muscles in your body. With your eyes closed, just let go, relaxing deeper and deeper.

Once you are fully relaxed, imagine in your mind's eye a television with a video player. In your hand you have a tape documenting all the important experiences of your early life. Put the tape into the player and watch.

The film begins by showing you as a child and the first experiences you can remember, then it moves forward to your first days in school. What were you like? See your parents, family, significant people in your life. Listen to what they are saying to you. You can stop the tape anytime you like, for a spot check or to focus in on an event or person in your life. Always notice how the person or event influenced you.

Now the tape moves slowly ahead through your various school experiences. Watch the major events and people right on up to age twenty or so. Take your time and get a good picture of your early life. When you've finished viewing the tape, open your eyes and slowly return to the present. Write down some of the impressions from your journey.

Selective Life Inventory

So far you've looked at your early life. Stage two focuses on a brief, selective inventory of where you have been in the past, and where you are now in respect to some key areas of living. Using a note pad, respond to each of the questions below. Don't write an essay, just write sufficiently detailed notes so that you know you have fully examined and responded to the question. Take your time, but don't dwell too long on each. About forty-five minutes to an hour should be time enough.

What have been my peak positive experiences?
These have been the most moving, inspiring, exhilarating, greatest times in your life. They have turned you on, made you feel fully alive, given you a sense of being in touch with things greater than yourself. They may have been momentary experiences (like a few minutes during a special ski run) or positive experiences of some duration (like the first few weeks in the life of your first child). Try to list as many as you can.

What things do I do well?

These are activities that you engage in, or have in the past. Take things you do well at present as your guide, but include things that you could still do well but may have abandoned. These need not be activities that you must do, but could just as well be seemingly playful things such as dancing, sailing, sports. This is a difficult job for many of us because we've been taught to be overly modest, thus often stressing what we do not do well. No one is watching, so make your list as comprehensive as possible.

What are my major personal strengths?

These are personal characteristics, abilities, traits of character, states of being and feeling, and aspects of yourself you value highly. Naturally, these are very personal judgments about your strengths — some people may value aggressiveness, while others might list that same trait as a personal weakness. If you think being a warm person is a strength, then list it. If you can organize things well and see this as a valued trait, include it. If you're very generous and feel this is good for you and others around you, list it. You may even find yourself listing the same trait later under personal weaknesses if you feel you are so generous that people take advantage of you.

What have been my key failure experiences?

This list should be a short one: first, because we're only talking about important failures; and second, because we're listing as failures only those things that we have wanted very much, tried hard to achieve, and failed to get. Don't include as failures regret or remorse that you didn't do something which you felt later you should have done.

What are my major personal weaknesses?

This category is in the same vein as the one above on personal strengths, only here it is tuned in to weakness rather than strength.

What have been my major goals in the past?

What goals and objectives have been motivating, given you power, energy, and the drive to keep going? Goals may include social and personal goals, broad life goals, work goals, and achievement goals.

What dreams do I want?

If I had a magic wand that would let me make two changes in myself at this very moment, what changes would I want?

Who Am I?

This stage is concerned with the present — what's going on with you right now. When this data is added to what you have retrieved about yourself in the first two segments, you'll be ready to think about the years ahead from a more solid base. This will make it much easier to define future goals with confidence and direction.

For this project you need a pen or pencil and ten 3"×5" cards or small slips of paper. What is called for here are ten different answers, one on each card, to the question, "Who Am I?" They can be a single word, a phrase, a sentence at most. They can be aspects of self (I'm gentle), roles (a daughter), attributes (a dreamer), traits (weak), characteristics (steady), states of feeling (confused), states of being (secure), or, as is usual, some of each. For best results, be as spontaneous as possible. Write your answers down as fast as you can — a few minutes is all you need. When you have finished, spread the slips before you so that you can see all of them. Put a #10 on the one that seems least important to you. Then look through them again, putting a #9 on the next least central to you. Continue on until you come to #1. This is the core of who you are, the aspect of you that seems most important. Take the cards and arrange them numerically in a pile with #1 on top and #10 at the bottom. Read them through once more, making sure the order you selected is your final choice.

Your Eulogy and Epitaph

How long has it been since you've let yourself have a full-blown fantasy of life, going all the way out to the very end? If you've done this recently, or ever, you're among the very few. It seems to be too painful, too frightening a venture for most — yet it can be an exciting and freeing experience, leading you on to greater growth and personal productivity. So take some time to reflect quietly about yourself, dream a bit, start some wishful fantasies going, and write a eulogy. Make it a eulogy that might be said of you at a service by a long-time, close friend who knew you very well. Make it a eulogy that you would like to have and that also has the possibility of being realized by the end of your life. Stretch your imagination to think of a future some years hence so that the eulogy is not one that could be written as of next week or next year.

At the end of the eulogy write an epitaph — a one liner. One written by a lifelong hypochondriac read: "See, I told you I was sick!"

Your eulogy should cover your whole life, what's happened up to now and what you hope might occur from now until your inevitable death. Here you can use your creativity to make your own predictions about the future.

Why shouldn't you make your own predictions? If your experience has been in any way like most, other people close to you have been predicting your future since you were a kid. "If you keep on the way you're going, you'll be a genius in mathematics." "You'll get shafted if you trust people too much." "If you don't finish school you'll never make it." "You should be a writer (businessman, engineer)." "Finally you've chosen the right career." "You've got such great potential as a _____, why don't you use it?"

Most people that I work with find writing their eulogy an unusual, exciting, and rewarding experience. It is a low-key way to make promises to yourself, partly in jest, partly serious, and it brings up all sorts of ways to think about the years ahead.

Future Life Inventory

Before starting this project, go back over all the data you've brought out up to now. You'll find it stimulating, revealing, and truly helpful in your work on the future life inventory. As you review the information you have gathered, you will probably recognize certain themes running throughout all the different parts of the exercise. You can use this information and your feelings and thoughts about it to good advantage in responding to the inventory.

The idea here is to project yourself five or six years into the future and respond to the questions as if you were already there. Don't write an essay, but make enough notes to be able to explore your responses fully. Think deeply about these questions. Take your time responding to them.

- What areas of my life and circumstances would I like to have changed or improved?

- What goals or objectives would I like to have realized?

- What particular strengths would I like to have developed more fully?

- What past personal characteristics would I like to be rid of?

- If I were told I had twelve months to live and that my vitality would remain as it is now until my death, how would I live those twelve months?

Now that you have completed the exercises and have some insights about your future, you will need to make some plans. Without some clarity about specific steps you wish to and where to begin, your Personal Strategic Plan possibly will be relegated to the pile of projects that never happen. Start by answering the questions below. Take your time and write as much as is needed to create a meaningful program.

- What particular activities and/or projects must I undertake over the next two years to bring about the changes I want in the next five or six years? Put a completion date with each.

- How will I have to change or grow to realize these future goals?

- Who will I have to take into account in making these changes? Why must I take them into consideration?

- Who can help me most in bringing about these changes? Make a comprehensive list.

Looking back at your work, what have you learned about thinking strategically and what new perceptions do you now have that will help you be more proactive in directing your life and career the way you want it?

Additional Information

Books

Profit Beyond Measure, Thomas Johnson and Anders Broms, Free Press, 2000. A guide to the way management thinks about and organizes work.

Simplified Strategic Planning, Robert Bradford and Peter Duncan, Chandler House Press, 1999. How to devise an appropriate strategy for your organization.

Jumping the Curve, Nicholas Imparatu and Oren Harari, Jossey-Bass, 1996. How to make significant, discontinuous leaps in thinking.

Life and Work, James Autry, Avon Business, 1994. Details the new strategy — practical and poetic, hard-headed and touching.

Leadership and the New Science, Margaret J. Wheatley, Barrett-Koehler Publishers, 1992. Connects current physics research, particularly chaos theory, with organizational behavior.

Visionary Leadership, Burt Nanus, Jossey-Bass, 1992. Shows why vision is the key to leadership and how any leader can bring a powerful new sense of direction to his organization.

The Fifth Discipline, Peter M. Senge, Doubleday/Currency, 1990. Describes the art and practice of the learning organization. The most talked-about management book of the last decade.

The Creative Brain, Ned Herrmann, Ned Herrmann Brain Books, 1989. How to develop untapped creative resources through understanding of the brain.

How to Interpret the Test for Chapter 1

This little test is by no means definitive, and no answer is completely right or wrong. It is intended to give you some insight into the style of thinking you favor. Many people make choices in both categories. As you will discover in this chapter and those that follow, the effective manager is able to use both styles of thinking and knows when to choose the appropriate one.

"Yes" answers to numbers 1, 2, 5, 8, and 10 are those most often favored by logical thinkers.

1. Facts are a perfect choice for judges and juries, for example. But, in dealing with people in organizations, a manager must also consider emotions and feelings.

2. Being thoughtful and focused is an essential part of leadership, but it sometimes causes a narrow view that does not consider all the possibilities. Inserting "often but not always" would help to bring balance.

5. This leads to hearing what you want to hear, not expanding the scope of your inquiry through new (different) ideas.

8. Rational and reliable needs to be offset by intuitive and spontaneous at times.

10. All human interaction involves feelings. If you keep yours under wraps you risk losing much of the real content.

"Yes" answers to numbers 3, 4, 6, 7, and 9 indicate use of a strategic style of thinking.

3. But first gather the facts.

4. Helpful in rounding out the picture.

6. Usually leads to more in-depth exploration

7. We all are. It's simply a question of owning it.

9. Honesty begets honesty, but you may not always like what you get back. Balance here is the keyword.

Chapter 2

How Do You Rate as a Collaborative Manager?

The ability to create a collaborative environment is an essential attribute for all managers. Test where you are by answering "Yes" or "No" to the questions. Then turn to the end of the chapter for the answers.

	Yes	No
1. People perform best when they have a say in the decisions that affect their work.	☐	☐
2. Most people are more concerned with acquiring material goods than they are with the quality of their work life.	☐	☐
3. Research shows that the best-run companies in America emphasize small groups, teamwork, and participation.	☐	☐
4. People like to be told exactly what to do rather than accept the risks that go with being autonomous.	☐	☐
5. Small companies or small divisions of big companies seem to have a natural advantage over huge, centralized organizations.	☐	☐
6. Working in a collaborative group environment is good for your health.	☐	☐
7. The way to keep workers in line is by making strict rules and using punishment liberally.	☐	☐
8. Being either an autocratic or democratic manager is less a matter of technique and more a matter of basic values.	☐	☐
9. Group decisions made by a well-developed team are often better than decisions made by the boss.	☐	☐
10. Managers who encourage participation at work often lead a more harmonious life outside work.	☐	☐

Chapter 2

Collaborating

The Nature of Collaboration

Douglas McGregor, in his 1960 book, *The Human Side of Enterprise*, told us with great clarity that people like to collaborate toward mutually identified goals, and that they perform best when they have a say in the decisions that affect their lives. That's a central issue, not only in this chapter, but in the entire understanding of how to manage people.

What workers mean when they say they want to collaborate on the job is simply this:

- Given a choice, they would be happier if they could be part of a group that works on the problems and projects in their area of the organization rather than having a supervisor make all the decisions.

- They would like the freedom and autonomy to do the job as they see it, usually as part of a team, instead of following a lock-step method dictated to them. The important issue is getting the work done.

- Access to information is essential to understanding. Workers would rather have facts than rumors. If organizational changes are indicated they would like to be part of both the decision and implementation processes.

- Free and open communication between management and workers is essential to a sense of belonging and to teamwork. Confronting situations directly and immediately rather than avoiding or putting things off creates bonding instead of the usual we/they polarization found so often in management practice. (More on this in Chapter 4.)

The collaborative group satisfies a deep need for intimacy in most people. In the group, people can really get close, share their problems, their feelings about management and, after awhile, their feelings about each other. Such groups have a healing quality. Research shows that when workers are part of ongoing, problem-solving groups, they tend to be absent less often, on time, healthier, have more energy, and accomplish more. Simply put, productivity improves and the bottom line improves.

The increase in individual energy is fascinating. When a collaborative work group nears the solution to a particularly difficult problem, the electricity in the room gets so high it's almost visible. Each person gets energized by the activity, and the energy gets passed around in a synergistic effect. We have been part of such groups and received a charge of energy from the activity that made it difficult to sleep that night.

It is very clear that collaborating teams are better for people and better for the company. Everybody wins.

One warning here. When we say "people" that means most people. There are always exceptions. A worker whose main interest was getting by until he could retire much preferred a beer on the way home to a team meeting discussing productivity. A purchasing clerk who was a loner type resisted every effort to include her in anything suggested. Pushing her into a collaborative group was useless.

Small Is Beautiful

There is research on organizational size as an important issue in productivity and humanizing the workplace. This is an interesting connection because it examines the natural advantage of the smaller company. Collaborative teams of six-to-ten persons optimize creativity, productivity, and worker satisfaction. For the majority of businesses in the U.S., this is the size of the total work force.

Many large corporations have studied the power of small groups and instituted the team concept. Now they are looking at an optimum plant size, too. The effectiveness of small groups lies in their ability to relate to the whole picture. If people don't see how their labor affects the end product, incentive is reduced and work becomes uninteresting. Economy of scale is being questioned and decentralization increasingly chosen.

All of this is a mighty plus for smaller firms. Large organizations must embrace the small-group concept to reduce alienation. In small businesses where that's usually not a problem, the addition of team building makes for some exceptional possibilities.

A Model Collaborative Team

How does a good collaborating team develop? How do its members act? What do they do? Let's look in on one. Our group is composed of six people (yours could be as small as three or four or as large as ten). Jack Gibb, one of the pioneer researchers in the field of team development, believed that six was just the right size for self-management. Gibb said that such self-regulated groups tend to outperform those managed by traditional methods.

Our group is composed of programmers working in an Information Technology department of a large oil company. Their task is to write and maintain programs for the company payroll system. This group of six programmers was formed a few months ago. At first, they met once a week for an hour or more. Since this group was started by management, a trainer was supplied to give guidance. The supervisor of this collaborative team is a well-balanced person with good technical skills. She likes her job and the people who work with her. She has no need for power. In the group she acts like any other member, freely expressing her opinion but never dominating. She usually goes along with the group's decisions, even when they don't agree with her own. She knows that even if the decision is not the best one (by her standards), it will probably work because the whole group is behind it. The only time she intervenes is to clarify company policy or to point out where a particular action might not fit in with other department activities. She uses her knowledge by being a source of information.

One of the early issues the team discusses is the number of programming errors that need correction in many of the older payroll programs. Finding scapegoats in earlier program developers or in other parts of the company would be easy enough, but the group members now trust each other and are comfortable enough to agree that a sizeable share of the problem results from their own errors. On deeper self-examination they agree that some lack sufficient familiarity with earlier programming languages, and their patches and corrections often are not enough to do the trick.

The team arrives at a solution: set up a self-administered training program. They can run some sessions themselves, using resources from within their own team. They will need assistance from members of other teams in the department as well. In a few months their technical knowledge has improved and they are able to reduce the time it takes them to detect and correct errors. They measure these changes and begin to set standards for future improvement.

In a later stage, the group gets together each morning for ten or fifteen minutes to talk about the day's schedule. They discuss programs that need attention, who should handle which projects, and how they can help each other. They are now a smoothly-functioning unit. From management's point of view, programs are maintained better, absenteeism and tardiness is negligible, and turnover is down substantially.

The view from inside the group is much improved as well. Where work was once routine, monotonous, and controlled by management, it is now autonomous and interesting. The source of motivation has shifted. Each member is desirous of doing the job well, where formerly, prods by management were needed to keep things moving. The atmosphere feels relaxed. Members remark about how good they feel, and they note that the incidence of colds and flu has dropped sharply.

From this example it is clear that organized, carefully-nurtured, autonomous work groups have many advantages. Such groups are more productive, create more respect for co-workers, inspire commitment to goals, and lower stress.

How to Become a Collaborative Manager

For some managers, collaboration comes easily. They usually feel pretty good about themselves, are trusting of others, tend not to be defensive, communicate easily and openly. Such managers are seen as "in person," not "in role." They don't need to invoke their titles to get things done. People want to work with them. It's fun. Their positive attitudes create self-fulfilling prophecies that result in excellent performance by themselves and their team managers.

Many young people come into the work force as naturals. They fit the description above. Left to do their work with reasonable autonomy, they would grow into successful business owners or managers. But they soon find that it's important to play the game, be devious, learn how to cheat a little, censor their communications, and behave according to the rules.

When we talk to these young people about the effective management styles described in this book, they understand immediately. It's their natural behavior, but they tell us they can't be that way on the job. Their boss rules with an iron fist, talks *at* them not *with* them, emphasizes being on time rather than getting the job done, chooses competition over collaboration. In order to protect themselves, these naturals begin to act like the managers of yesterday, perpetuating an anachronistic, ineffective system.

If you're one of the naturals, support your instincts by building a solid theoretical framework. Learn all you can about effective management styles so you will never question who's right. Resist the pressures to conform to the old model. Just keep focused on what's right for you and follow your intuition.

If you are a business owner and a natural, hurray for you and for the people lucky enough to be part of your company. Your challenge is to learn everything you can about ways to make your personal style company policy. In your meetings you will want to talk about people processes (how we are working together as a team). Take time to solidify your group. Make sure they understand that it's okay to speak up, to be creative. Encourage open communication; keep everybody informed about company activities. Live your vision.

What if you are from the carrot-and-stick, and run-a-tight-ship school? Well, you can join in the pleasures of collaborative management, too. Your present body of knowledge is based on what you were taught. Anything learned can be changed — but you must really become a believer in the new ethic. Many managers are so change-resistant they won't read or discuss possibilities for growth. They are fearful about what would happen if they considered a new style and that always leads to retaining tight control, the antithesis of collaboration.

Begin your change process by playing "as if." Decide to work with your employees in a collaborative way, then do it just as if it were natural.

Once you are started, you will find from your own experience that working as a team member is rewarding, fun, and a lot easier than traditional management. After awhile the new behavior will become integrated into your style, replacing the old. Done with conviction, your new management behavior will be perceived as honest.

One of the big problems in most management training is teaching "techniques." People learn that if they pat a few backs now and then and give employees the feeling of participation, they are satisfying the description of a collaborative manager. That's being a wolf in sheep's clothing and you will always be discovered. Cosmetic changes are worse than no changes at all because they are basically dishonest. Workers always see through manipulative behavior.

Making the change to a new style of management often means a change in how you view the world and your relationship to it. It means alterations in your value system. No training session is going to do that. You must really want to change from the inside out. Tall order, you say. We have watched hundreds of business owners and managers do just that — completely change their thinking and style — and come out at the end so much more effective and happy with their lives that they become the catalyst for change in others. Once you have experienced being with your employees in the decision-making process, rather than handing down orders, you will discard the old style forever.

Now that you understand the importance of becoming a true believer, here are some helpful hints and information. Remember: these are to be used for your personal growth, not as tools to get your employees moving. Watch it! If used manipulatively, these tidbits will turn around and bite you.

- A collaborative environment includes you as a collaborator. You join the group as a member, not as the leader. As a member, you can give your opinion, be a source of information that will assist the process, in fact do anything except demand obedience. Once you take charge, the whole thing goes back to square one. We will give you a guarantee: the decisions made by the group will be the best for the company over the long haul. Even if they make a choice that you feel is not the best, they will make it work because they have a commitment to the result.

- Commitment is important — everyone needs to buy into the team process. Don't expect that to happen overnight. Spotted leopards are always suspect when they start acting like pussy cats. If you have been authoritarian, suddenly switching to a democratic style is likely to raise more than eyebrows. Don't expect people to fall into line immediately — they won't. But if you give them clear messages about your intent, over many months they will become convinced and make their commitment to the team.

- The decision to become collaborative has profound implications for the future of your company or group. Try not to experiment with the idea. Once started, it can't easily be stopped. When people in organizations find that their deepest desires are being met through working together as a team, disbanding the team or cancelling meetings causes a feeling of deprivation way beyond the antagonism at the beginning. If you don't have a serious commitment to the process, don't start!

- Once you are practicing teamwork, don't cancel scheduled meetings of the group. When you substitute some other activity for the meeting, you are putting out signals that the team is not important to you.

- As pointed out earlier, not everyone is a prospect for collaboration. A good way to ensure a productive group is to make participation voluntary. If the group is successful and people are enjoying themselves, most of those who stayed out will clamor to get in.

- Be prepared for lots of questions. You have opened the door to autonomy and equality. Questions never openly raised before will surface now. The way to handle all questions is with total candor. Try not to have privileged information, but if some information is best not made public, say so. If you don't know an answer, admit it. If you are asked how you feel about a subject, respond with your true feelings. This is the best time to be honest and come clean. Any discomfort you experience in the beginning will give way to the deep sense of ease that comes from not being secretive or lying.

- If you are only half a believer, but you would like to get started on a collaborative environment anyhow, here's another way: start by telling your people the real story — that you have always believed in the old managerial concept of controlling and directing, but that you would like to try the new way. Encourage them to get involved, and to let you know when they feel you are being authoritarian. If you never punish anyone for being honest with you, your people will help you learn. (See Chapter 4 for more discussion about open communications.)

- Ignoring the group's recommendations is the kiss of death. Group decisions must be acted on. That doesn't necessarily mean implemented. You still retain the right to overrule something if, in your wisdom, it will seriously damage the company. But explain why. Don't ignore anything. Give positive signals to the group about how you value them.

- Learn to be more trusting. Your group is probably composed of people you hired because you had confidence in their ability. They are there because you believe in them. If neither of these statements is true for you, be merciful and fire or transfer those who don't fit. Give them an opportunity to grow in their own way. *A good manager is a supportive coach and a developer of people.*

- Start backing up your change process with more knowledge. Take some classes in organizational behavior. Read books on the subject. Go to seminars. Talk with managers in other companies about their success with collaboration. Whatever stage your career is in, continuing education is essential. You can't succeed in this fast-track business world without keeping current with your industry and the business world in general.

- If you start collaboration at the workplace, it will probably carry over into your home life. You can use this safe environment for trying out new ways of being. Surface some problems family members have been avoiding and work through a solution that you can all buy into. Working out family problems together will put new joy into your relationships. One couple calls a family meeting once a week. Everybody attends. After dinner the dishes are removed and whatever is on people's minds is put on the table. Everything is okay to discuss — how daddy behaved yesterday, how junior is not helping out, how everyone feels. If all families would conduct regular, open meetings with the same zeal they put into other activities, many psychotherapists would go out of business. It's that powerful.

- Have a full measure of patience. All groups run into problems in the formative stage. Everyone is trying to find a place for himself or herself, goals need clarification, structure is being designed, and a general tenseness may exist. Expect this and allow for it. Being and working together over time will bring relaxation and cohesiveness.

- When you begin to feel comfortable, open up. Become more risk-taking in your interventions. Say how you feel about yourself and the group. Be as open and honest as you would like others to be. This is a key issue. Openness and honesty are central to a group's success.

- Allow and participate in frank, open criticism, but not in an attacking way. Make criticism a constructive method for removing obstacles to getting the job done. Conflict is a natural part of organizational and interpersonal behavior. Burying it does not make it go away — it hangs around and comes out in inappropriate ways. The best way to handle conflict is to acknowledge it and deal with it thoroughly until it's resolved. Unresolved conflict in groups and in all relationships is a barrier to growth.

- Be supportive. This is a vital characteristic of a good group member. Accept suggestions, information, and criticism openly. Withhold judgment until all the evidence is in. Assist in developing sound ideas with which you agree. Show respect for all contributions and even if you don't agree, make sure everyone gets heard.

- Foster cooperation rather than competitiveness. Be on the lookout for win-lose situations and try to find solutions where everyone wins. Losers often become saboteurs of the group goal.

- If you are giving feedback (expressing yourself) to another person, watch for judgmental statements. You can recognize judgments in words such as good, bad, should, shouldn't, right, wrong. It's much better to express your own emotional reactions by describing yourself as sad, excited, confused, angry, afraid, relieved. When you point out another person's behavior, judgments can get you into trouble, but if you simply state your own feelings, there's an opening for discussion or sharing. You can temper things even further if you state that the problem may be yours, or that what you are saying is purely your own reaction.

- Watch out for speaking past other members — showing how smart you are or using technical language. Be personal.

- The group deals with the agenda it has decided on, but there are often hidden agendas. The other agendas belong to individual members. They may concern interpersonal conflicts, loyalty to another group, personal fears, or problems with the process of the group itself. Any or all of these issues may become apparent at any time, and they must be dealt with if the basic issues of the group are to be resolved. By staying alert, you will recognize the introduction of side issues, stalling tactics, and interference with group procedures. When all does not go smoothly, you can be sure there are hidden agendas at work. The way you can help the group is by being aware of your own hidden agendas. When you are, speak up and admit them. Be free in expressing your concerns, feelings, attitudes. Open behavior models the way for others.

- Subgroups often occur within the large group. Members will line up on one issue, then alignment will shift on a new matter. But, when permanent cliques form, the group is in danger. This signals that matters concerning the group are being dealt with on the outside. Watch that you don't align yourself with a clique, and never discuss group business in the hallways or in the restroom. The place to discuss group affairs is in the group meetings.

- Be sure that group goals are clear and have been established by the group itself. Then work hard for team objectives and expect others to do the same. This builds group loyalty, which is organizational cement.

- Decision making in groups seems to take a long time, but such a process considers the worth of each individual. Everyone gets involved, everyone inputs until a way is found that fits the entire group. This process knits the group more tightly together and assures the decision will work because it belongs to everyone.

- Important in organizing or being in a successful group is the understanding that expertise is not the most important value. It is important that you participate in the group openly as a whole person, being and showing who you are. Our conditioning teaches us to hide behind our roles and our head knowledge. This is not to denigrate intellectual understanding of what you are doing — it is essential, but without being a feeling, caring person, knowledge is of little help in a group situation.

Making Value Shifts

Start thinking and acting in new ways, using this checklist to monitor your progress. A manager in a value shift from an authoritarian model to a collaborative model moves in these directions:

- From focus on role to focus on relationships between people;

- From being impersonal to being personal;

- From screening responses and being professional to being spontaneous and sharing;

- From concern for straightening everyone up to concern for the growth
of individuals and development of the group;

- From being evaluative and making judgments to describing personal
feelings and perceptions;

- From focus on the limitations of employees to focus on their strength
and growth potential;

- From being fearful, cautious, and controlling to being trusting, adven-
turesome, and free;

- From being linear and rigid in relationships with subordinates to being
intuitive and following a gut-feeling for what to do.

All you need to know is already inside you. You need simply uncover the
essential you. Being a real person means being imperfect, searching, trying new ways, making mistakes, recovering, and trying again. Experts
hide behind their knowledge and are not available for human contact.
Real people get the maximum from a group experience and give the
most, both to the content and process of a team.

A Checklist for Collaborative Management

Being an effective manager of people requires eyes and ears beyond the
usual two each. Use this checklist to help expand your awareness.

1. Check with the team. Before initiating any action that affects the
organization, I run it by the team to get their concurrence and support.

2. Encourage feedback. I behave in ways that allow my people to talk to
me about anything, including my management style. I encourage them
to openly critique any and all issues, problems, and differences among
themselves — always focusing on the activity, never on the person.

3. Focus on collaboration, not competition. We compete with other
companies. Internally we support each other and work as a team.

4. Share a vision. We have a common company (or departmental) perspective of our goal. We affirm this direction in everything we do.

5. Remember that entrepreneurs are everywhere. Entrepreneurship is not
just at the top. I encourage new ideas and new methods at every level.

6. Respond affirmatively. The first response to any proposal is, "Yes, let's give it a try." I find reasons to support the idea, not reject it.

7. List process as our most important product. I pay as much attention to the quality of our interaction on the team as I do to the quality of our product or service.

8. Join with others. I do not act as a parent, guardian, or boss or take any other superior role. I join others as a member of the team. Joining does not absolve me of responsibility. It simply makes others responsible, too.

9. Let the group decision stand. If there is solid consensus, I go along with the team, even if its decision is different from the one I had in mind.

10. Empower others. Rather than holding on to power, I allow others to be autonomous. In setting them free, I free myself and the entire organization.

Additional Information

Books

People in Charge, Robert Rehm, Hawthorne Press, 2000. A step-by-step design for self-managing workplaces.

The Web of Inclusion, Sally Hegesen, Doubleday, 1995. A model of collaborative management.

No Contest: The Case Against Competition, Alfie Kohn, Houghton Mifflin, 1986. Kohn argues that competition is inherently destructive.

The Art of Japanese Management, Richard T. Pascale and Anthony G. Athos, Simon and Schuster, 1981. The best insights into participative techniques started in the United States, were picked up by the Japanese, and are now back home.

People at Work, Pehr G. Gyllenhammar, Addison-Wesley, 1977. The president of Volvo describes the dramatic change in a major automobile plant. People work in small groups, getting a chance to influence their working environment.

The Human Side of Enterprise, Douglas McGregor, McGraw-Hill Book Co., 1960. This is the classic that gave us Theory X and Theory Y. Must reading for anyone who wants to understand the background of participative management.

Resources

The Extension Department of your local university offers group experiences and leadership laboratories.

How to Interpret the Test for Chapter 2

The answers to 1, 3, 5, 6, 8, 9, and 10 are all "Yes," based on the many studies of people at work.

The answer to number 2 is "No." Polls show that, for the majority of people, the quality of their life is more important than what they can buy. The percentage who think this way keeps rising.

The answer to number 4 is a qualified "No." Most working people resent explicit directions. They prefer to use some of their own creativity.

If you answered "Yes" to number 7, you may be managing with a long-outdated style. Punishment as a way of controlling the workforce has been ineffective for many years.

Chapter 3

Test Your Readiness for Team Building

Building a team takes time, commitment, and readiness. Work through the questions and find out if you are ready, then find the answers on the last page of this chapter.

	Yes	No
1. Do you feel comfortable sharing decision making and leadership with your subordinates?	☐	☐
2. Do you prefer working in a collaborative atmosphere over running a tight ship yourself?	☐	☐
3. To achieve your goals for the company or your work unit, is it important for you to have a high level of interdependence?	☐	☐
4. Do you feel members of your group can make decisions in the best interests of the company?	☐	☐
5. Are you willing to receive feedback on your performance from your group?	☐	☐
6. Do you believe your group needs to meet regularly to establish goals, make decisions, and implement action?	☐	☐
7. Do you think it important to bring up and work through sensitive interpersonal issues?	☐	☐
8. Do you need the best ideas of your staff to meet the challenges of a changing environment?	☐	☐
9. Are you willing to invest company time in forming a team to accomplish your objectives?	☐	☐
10. Can you act as a facilitator in the group, allowing leadership to pass around as appropriate?	☐	☐
11. Can you deal with conflict directly, rather than sweep it under the rug?	☐	☐
12. Do you trust your staff sufficiently to allow them the freedom to make a mistake?	☐	☐

Chapter 3

Team Building

A Team Is More Than a Group

Working with others on a collaborative venture, helping make the decisions that affect his or her own work life — these are central issues for the contemporary American worker. An additional step in this process raises the group concept to an even higher level — being part of a *team*. Three things distinguish a team from a group:

1. A team has common goals that everyone clearly accepts and a real need to work together to accomplish these goals.

2. A team has invested substantial time, usually in formal training, to learn how to work together.

3. Trained teams learn to focus on process (how members interact) as well as on content (the assigned task).

The distinction is important. Many group opportunities are available, but few team ones. The word "team" is bandied about in organizations, but these "teams" usually turn out to be informal work groups. Teams are intentional. They are put together with the idea that they will stay together over an extended period of time. They have a specific, long-term objective.

At the shop-floor level, a well-designed, total-quality management program meets the team criteria if the personnel have adequate training in team concepts and if the members continually examine their own process in addition to dealing with task issues. Some of the activities of such a team are described in Chapter 2.

An executive group that meets regularly to direct the plans of the company can meet the team criteria if it engages in frequent team-building activities free from task pressure, and if it stops to examine and correct its process as it proceeds with its work.

At other levels of management, the same criteria apply. Groups that gather to exchange information are certainly helpful, but to produce results the members need to focus on and improve their interactions with each other.

Well-developed teams do not promote sweetness and light. They encourage conflict and differences of opinion, but they do it in a way that leaves everyone feeling good. If you are observing a work unit in any organization and wondering whether it is a team or just a group, you might test for these characteristics:

- Do members really listen, trying to understand the points of view, objectives, and preferred solutions of others?
- Are people being candid — saying what they want to say all of the time rather than being guarded?
- To what extent are members trying to find innovative, mutually acceptable solutions rather than fighting for their own individual preferences?
- How well can each member state the position of another (see the issue from another person's point of view)?
- Are conflicts settled by win-lose confrontation, negotiation and compromise, or creative problem-solving using consensus?
- When the going gets rough, do they use a third party to help them find a mutually acceptable solution?
- Once a solution is reached, is everybody really buying in, or does residual hostility remain that will inhibit its implementation?
- Do power struggles interfere or is everyone focused on organizational results?
- When they reach a decision, does everyone join in the implementation and follow-through?

Groups that have not gone through (and do not reinforce) team building usually perform their assigned tasks poorly. When divisive forces intrude, loyalty is low, and when group members have poor interactive skills, they can be expected to produce poor results.

Team building has as a core issue the development of trust. In low-trust groups, interpersonal problems get in the way of finding solutions. Members use much of their creative energy to protect themselves. In high-trust groups, members feel comfortable about being open and above-board and all the energy of the team is available to solve the problem.

Building a team begins with a state of mind. Owners, presidents, or managers who attempt to build a team must understand the importance of collaboration and be willing to let go of power. They must be free of the negative behaviors they are trying to purge from the group. They need to come to the very first meeting willing to spend the necessary time to work issues through, and be committed to never sweeping anything under the rug.

Members must understand the benefits of teamwork — not only better company results, but opportunities for personal growth and enjoyment. Being part of a smoothly functioning team is one of the most rewarding of human experiences. Far from reducing everyone to a common level, as happens in many undifferentiated, poorly focused groups, a team fosters and nourishes individualism and helps to clarify individual identity.

A Model Team

Earlier we mentioned the importance of Douglas McGregor's work to our present concept of collaborative management. He identifies the characteristics of an effective work team.[1]

- The atmosphere, which can be sensed in a few minutes of observation, tends to be informal, comfortable, relaxed. There are no obvious tensions. It is a working atmosphere in which people are involved and interested. There are no signs of boredom.

- There is a lot of discussion in which virtually everyone participates, but it remains pertinent to the task of the group. If the discussion gets off the subject, someone will bring it back in short order.

---

1. Douglas McGregor, *The Human Side of Enterprise* (New York: McGraw-Hill Book Co., 1960), pp. 232–235.

- The task or the objective of the group is well understood and accepted by the members. There will have been free discussion of the objective at some point until it was formulated in such a way that the members of the group could commit themselves to it.

- The members listen to each other! The discussion does not have the quality of jumping from one idea to another unrelated one. Every idea is given a hearing. People do not appear to be afraid of being foolish by putting forth a creative thought even if it seems fairly extreme.

- There is disagreement. The group is comfortable with this and shows no signs of having to avoid conflict or to keep everything on a place of sweetness and light. Disagreements are not suppressed or overridden by premature group action. The reasons are carefully examined, and the group seeks to resolve them rather than to dominate the dissenter.

On the other hand, there is no "tyranny of the minority." Individuals who disagree do not appear to be trying to dominate the group or to express hostility. Their disagreement is an expression of a genuine difference of opinion, and they expect a hearing to find a solution.

Sometimes there are basic disagreements which cannot be resolved. The group finds it possible to live with them, accepting them but not permitting them to block its efforts. Under some conditions, actions will be deferred to permit further study of an issue between the members.

On other occasions, where the disagreement cannot be resolved and action is necessary, it will be taken but with open caution and recognition that the action may be subject to later reconsideration.

- Most decisions are reached by a kind of consensus in which it is clear that everybody is in general agreement and willing to go along. However, there is little tendency for individuals who oppose the action to keep their opposition private and thus let an apparent consensus mask real disagreement. Formal voting is at a minimum; the group does not accept a simple majority as a proper basis for action.

- Criticism is frequent, frank, and relatively comfortable. There is little evidence of personal attack, either openly or in a hidden fashion. The criticism has a constructive flavor in that it is oriented toward removing an obstacle that faces the group and prevents it from getting the job done.

- People are free in expressing their feelings as well as their ideas both on the problem and on the group's operation. There is little pussyfooting;

there are few "hidden agendas." Everybody appears to know quite well how everybody else feels about any matter under discussion.

- When action is taken, clear assignments are made and accepted.

- The chairperson of the group does not dominate it nor, on the contrary, does the group defer unduly to him or her. In fact, as one observes the activity, it is clear that the leadership shifts from time to time, depending on the circumstances. Different members, because of their knowledge or experience, are in a position at various times to act as "resources" for the group. The members utilize them in this fashion and they occupy leadership roles while they are thus being used. There is little evidence of a struggle for power as the group operates. The issue is not who controls but how to get the job done.

- The group is self-conscious about its own operations. Frequently, it will stop to examine how well it is doing or what may be interfering with its operation. The problem may be a matter of procedure, or it may be an individual whose behavior is interfering with the accomplishment of the group's objectives. Whatever it is, it gets open discussion until a solution is found.

I suggest you use this as a checklist for your team-building efforts and to monitor your progress. If you develop your team along these lines, you will have few problems.

Process Versus Task

For any team, the task is the content of the meeting — what you are there to work on. Most businesspeople get fairly good at handling the task. If you examine meetings that don't work, you will quickly discover it's not because the members can't handle the task, but because the members can't work together toward a mutually agreeable solution. How they go about the task, how they join each other, relate to their differences, communicate — all these are aspects of the process.

All successful teams work on their internal process as hard as they work on the task. They don't blindly charge into the problem. They try to discover how things are going in the group, encourage full participation, really listen to each other and try to reach consensus rather than majority rule. In the beginning, it's a good idea to monitor your team's process in two ways.

1. When you see one person taking over the team, people not listening, people dropping out, or any activity that slows or interferes with the team's process, call a momentary halt. Ask the team members how they feel about the way things are going. They may be reluctant to deal with issues at first, but as the group develops, they will identify the blocks and decide how to handle them.

2. At the end of every meeting allow fifteen minutes for a process discussion. Never miss this part of the session. Simply ask, "How did we do today?" Eventually, team members will realize that they are going to be discussing the process and this will increase their awareness of that process during the regular task part of the meeting.

Consider a Consultant

If your team works well together, if your staff feels it is safe to be honest and speak up, and if they are all committed to work together as a team, then team building may function as an integral part of your regular work. If you are having problems in these areas, though, you may want to consider bringing in someone impartial from outside your group, or even your company. Choose someone who has training and experience in organizational development, someone who understands and can help you implement the concepts in this book. A good source is the behavioral science staff in the school of business at your local university. One of the prime reasons for bringing in somebody from the outside is that, as the boss, you may unknowingly be part of the problem. It's no news that many people have difficulty relating to those they perceive to be in authority. This can be particularly true of those employees who come from organizational cultures where the boss' word is law. An outside consultant has no axe to grind. He or she can give unbiased, straightforward feedback to all members of the team, including you! Good consultants will leave you with the capability and confidence to continue your team's development on your own. They will train you in the subtle art of facilitating a group while still remaining a part of it, or in the even more subtle art of letting somebody else facilitate while you remain a member of the group. Along with your team, you will learn problem diagnosis, planning, and process observation. With a consultant you can plan an offsite, several-day development program that can give you and your team the basics to build upon for the future.

Team-Building Strategy

At the very beginning, bring together everyone whose work connects them with each other. Discuss what you intend to do, accept questions, and answer frankly. Get a commitment from them to join the team.

The best bet is to hold an initial two or three day off-site process training session with a consultant. Getting away from the everyday pressures of work and being together constantly helps to build cohesiveness.

If time and expense are a problem, hold a series of local meetings. Perhaps you can start with an all-day Saturday session and then continue the following week with a two- or three-hour session at the end of each day. It's important to get as much time as possible to learn together. This learning keeps everyone focused, emphasizes the importance of the meeting, and gets the process off to a fast start.

Once your initial team building session is over, you can begin regularly scheduled task meetings, integrating your new process knowledge into the way you conduct the meetings. Here are some things to consider.

- The team's first task is to identify its concerns, problems, or issues. Often these will come out of the discussion, but you may need to add to them and help define some of them. Having issues and goals crystal clear is very important.

- Starting with the first regular meeting and in every meeting thereafter, allow time to analyze the team's process. It's easy to drift back into focus on the task only. When participation lags or members express dissatisfaction with the results of a meeting, that's a sign that it's time to discuss the process.

- Watch for team members smoothing ruffled feathers and pouring oil on troubled waters. If everything looks calm and peaceful all the time, a good possibility exists that conflicts are being buried, not resolved.

- Long-standing teams often recycle through some of their phases. When all seems to have been worked out, new interpersonal problems may erupt. This is only a signal that the members are integrating their prior learning and are prepared to go deeper into resolving issues between themselves. If no one panics, this can be the phase that really solidifies the team.

- Be prepared for more innovative and risky decisions from the team than individual members would make. Research shows that, contrary to popular belief, teams tend to foster risk-taking.

- Avoid majority voting. This creates winners and losers, a sure way to reduce the team's long-term effectiveness. Try to work toward consensus, reaching a decision that all the members can agree on.

- Encourage participation by everyone, but do it so that no one feels coerced. People become involved when they perceive support in the team, when they feel safe, when their views are valued, when there is no fear of ridicule, and when interpersonal issues are dealt with in a nonthreatening, nonpunitive manner.

- Watch out for your negative body language. Even though you may not express your disapproval in words, shaking your head, raising your eyebrows, or scowling gives the same message.

When you build the members of your staff into a team, you multiply their effectiveness. Building a collaborative team is the best way to improve the quality of work life for team members and to improve the bottom line for your company

Establishing Meeting Guidelines

The guides and exercises that follow are designed to help you build a cohesive, effective team. Remember, no team is perfect; development takes time and patience. Start by devoting several sessions to just being together and talking about how you can function as a unit. Allow ample time for whatever comes up, but try not to start working on company issues until you feel comfortable with each other. Just having dinner as a team and sharing conversation in the evening is an effective way to achieve this. Informal camaraderie draws people together.

Once you start working on tasks, you will need to continually monitor your process. I suggest you devote at least fifteen or twenty minutes at the end of each meeting to a self-evaluation. Start with the question "How did we do today as a team?" Then take it from there.

Another good idea: If the team is large enough to spare one person each meeting from participating in the task, appoint a process observer. This job should rotate through the group. The observer will watch the team's process and take notes. A Process Observer's Guide is furnished in this section. At the end of the meeting, the observer gives feedback to the group on how they functioned in various categories. The team can then use these comments to improve its performance next time. A copy of How to Be a Good Team Member, later in this chapter, can be a reminder of appropriate behavior.

One last word before you begin your big adventure. Committed teams are usually able to work out their problems and improve how they function without much guidance. You can help things along by organizing procedures using the materials provided. Beyond that, you can be most effective as a member of the group, allowing leadership to pass among the members. If you allow autonomy, the group will succeed. I call this "trusting the process." Even when things seem like they'll never work out, hang in there with the others. Your trust will pay off in a smoothly functioning team.

Team Development Scale

William G. Dyer developed this scale to measure the progress of a team.[2] Your team should use it whenever you wish to sense how team members feel and to supplement the process observer's report.

1. To what extent do I feel a real part of the team?

    1 – Completely a part all the time.

    2 – A part most of the time.

    3 – On the edge, sometimes in, sometimes out.

    4 – Generally outside, except for one or two short periods.

    5 – On the outside, not really a part of the team.

2. How safe is it in this team to be at ease, relaxed, and myself?

    1 – I feel perfectly safe to be myself, they won't hold mistakes against me.

    2 – I feel most people would accept me if I were completely myself, but there are some I am not sure about.

    3 – Generally, you have to be careful what you say or do in this team.

    4 – I am quite fearful about being completely myself in this team.

    5 – People would be fools to be themselves in this team.

3. To what extent do I feel "under wraps," that is, have private thoughts, unspoken reservations, or unexpressed feelings and opinions that I have not felt comfortable bringing out into the open?

    1 – Almost completely under wraps.

    2 – Under wraps many times.

---

2. William G. Dyer, *Team Building: Issues and Alternatives*, Copyright 1977, Addison Wesley Publishing Co., Inc. Reading, MA. Pp. 68–70. Reprinted with permission.

3. (continued)

   3 – Slightly more free and expressive than under wraps.

   4 – Quite free and expressive much of the time.

   5 – Almost completely free and expressive.

4. How effective are we, in our team, in getting out and using the ideas, opinions, and information of all team members in making decisions?

   1 – We don't really encourage everyone to share their ideas, opinions, and information with the team in making decisions.

   2 – Only the ideas, opinions, and information of a few members are really known and used in making decisions.

   3 – Sometimes we hear the views of most members before making decisions and sometimes we disregard most members.

   4 – A few are sometimes hesitant about sharing their opinions, but we generally have good participation in making decisions.

   5 – Everyone feels his or her ideas, opinions, and information are given a fair hearing before decisions are made.

5. To what extent are the goals the team is working toward understood and to what extent do they have meaning for you?

   1 – I feel extremely good about the goals of our team.

   2 – I feel fairly good, but some things are not too clear or meaningful.

   3 – A few things we are doing are clear and meaningful.

   4 – Much of the activity is not clear or meaningful to me.

   5 – I really do not understand or feel involved in the goals of the team.

6. How well does the team work at its task?

   1 – Coasts, loafs, makes no progress.

   2 – Makes a little progress, most members loaf.

   3 – Progress is slow, spurts of effective work.

   4 – Above average in progress and pace of work.

   5 – Works well, achieves definite progress.

7. Our planning and the way we operate as a team is largely influenced by:

   1 – One or two team members.

2 – A clique.

3 – Shifts from one person or clique to another.

4 – Shared by most of the members, some left out.

5 – Shared by all members of the team.

8. What is the level of responsibility for work in our team?

1 – Each person assumes personal responsibility for getting work done.

2 – A majority of the members assume responsibility for getting work done.

3 – About half assume responsibility, about half do not.

4 – Only a few assume responsibility for getting work done.

5 – Nobody (except perhaps one) really assumes responsibility for getting work done.

9. How are differences or conflicts handled in our team?

1 – Differences or conflicts are denied, suppressed, or avoided at all cost.

2 – Differences or conflicts are recognized, but remain unresolved mostly.

3 – Differences or conflicts are recognized and some attempts are made to work them through by some members, often outside the team meetings.

4 – Differences and conflicts are recognized and some attempts are made to deal with them in our team.

5 – Differences and conflicts are recognized and the team usually is working them through satisfactorily.

10. How do people relate to the team leader, chairperson, or "boss"?

1 – The leader dominates the team and people are often fearful or passive.

2 – The leader tends to control the team, although people generally agree with the leader's direction.

3 – There is some give and take between the leader and the team members.

10. (continued)

    4 – Team members relate easily to the leader and usually are able to influence leader decisions.

    5 – Team members respect the leader, but they work together as a unified team with everyone participating and no one dominant.

11. What suggestions do you have for improving our team functioning?

How to Be a Good Team Member

You are a vital part in the success of the team. The team members solve problems and make decisions. The team must lead itself and success or failure depends on the efforts of each participant. The following are ways of being in the group and the responsibilities you must assume to build and sustain your team.

1. Be a good listener. Give others your full attention and be open to what's being said. Don't be thinking of your reply. Respect your fellow team members. Don't distract them by making side remarks, whispering, or cutting anyone off.

2. Be honest and open. Show your underlying feelings. If each team member tries to do this regularly and it becomes a group norm, you will be able to deal with any contingency.

3. Accept other people's needs and desires. Don't judge. See differences as just that — not right or wrong.

4. Be positive. Keep an open mind. Don't evaluate an idea before it has had a chance to be developed. Look for the positive aspects of every suggestion.

5. Don't be defensive. Accept criticism as something to build on, not as a personal attack.

6. Learn to take the initiative. Express your own ideas and act on your own impulses rather than wait for someone else to begin.

7. Become more sensitive to the different ways people communicate, which involves much more than the words being said. Watch facial expressions, tone of voice, gestures, and posture.

8. Take a risk. Say how you feel. Try something new.

9. See the uniqueness in each of your team members. Try to build relationships.

10. Be trusting — of yourself, of others, and of the group process. You will find yourself being perceived as trustworthy.

11. Be responsible. You are one hundred percent responsible for getting what you want from the team and for ensuring the team's success. If you are fully invested in each moment of the team's work, you will encourage others to do the same. The result will be a hefty increase in your own energy and personal well-being.

Process Observer's Guide

At every regular meeting of the team, one member is chosen to be the process observer. This duty is passed around, each member taking a turn. The observer does not participate in the group. His or her job is to observe how the group is functioning and to give feedback to the members at the end of the session or during the session if requested.

The observer watches the team-play and the individual members' contributions. The form below serves as a guide, but feel free to add other observations of your own. At the end of the meeting the observer provides feedback to the group for acceptance or discussion. Remember that perceptions of what happens in a group vary among members, so different views are to be expected. If the observer offers views not as fact but as perception, then the team can discuss the offering freely. The important point is that the team talks about its process and that team members have a chance to alter their behavior if doing so will improve the performance of the team.

Group Atmosphere

1. Were people involved and interested? Did the interaction seem like drudgery or pleasure? Were members getting satisfaction from being in the group?

2. Were people collaborating or competing?

3. Was the atmosphere congenial or unfriendly?

4. What happened when a conflict occurred? Was it dealt with or was it swept under the rug?

Participation

1. Did some members participate more than others? Who?

2. Who participated least? How were they treated?

3. Were contributions on target, or did they lead the group away from the issue?

4. How well did the leader serve the group?

Influence

1. Who carried the ball most often?

2. Did rivalries arise? How were they handled?

Procedures

1. How was the agenda for the meeting set? How well was it adhered to? Did other agendas show up?

2. Did the group stay on track?

3. Were decisions reached by consensus or by a majority vote? How did this affect the group?

4. Did anyone take control by introducing a topic or making a decision for the group?

5. Were subgroups formed? How did this affect the process?

6. What did not get dealt with because it might be too risky?

Ground Rules

1. How well did the group follow the meeting guidelines?

2. Did anyone call attention to the guidelines when needed? What happened?

Additional Information

Books

The Complete Idiot's Guide to Team Building, Arthur R. Pell, MacMillan Distribution, 1999. Funny title, but jam-packed with great ideas, helpful hints, and how-to's about working in teams.

Executive Marbles and Other Team Building Activities, Sam W. Sikes, Learning Unlimited Corporation, 1998. Meaningful activities to increase team effectiveness.

The Wisdom of Teams, J.R. Katzenbach and Douglas K. Smith, Harvard Business School Press, 1993. How to create the high-performance organization.

Team players and Teamwork: The New Competitive Business Strategy, Glenn N. Parker, Jossey-Bass, 1991. Walks you through the team-building process.

Empowered Teams, Wellins, Byham, Wilson, Jossey-Bass, 1991. How to empower employees with a spirit of ownership, responsibility, and authority.

Building Productive Teams, Glenn H. Varney, Jossey-Bass, 1989. Provides detail on each of the issues discussed in this chapter.

Resources

For a consultant in your area, contact a local business school of a major university. Ask for the behavioral faculty. Interview several faculty members until you find one with whom the chemistry feels just right.

How to Interpret the Test for Chapter 3

If you answered "Yes" to nine or more questions, you are probably ready to begin a team-building program. If you find you are not ready for this step, read through Chapter 3, then go on to other chapters. You may find that starting in another area will give you the confidence to come back and work on team development.

Chapter 4

How Do You Rate as a Communicator?

Organizational communication is an interpersonal matter. Check your effectiveness by answering "Yes" or "No" to these statements, then check the last page of this chapter.

	Yes	No
1. Most problems between people are caused by failures in communications.	☐	☐
2. People's cosmology (view of the world) conditions everything they hear.	☐	☐
3. Confronting a subordinate on any issue requires that you just stick with the facts.	☐	☐
4. Watching body language and sensing what is going on is equally important as listening to the words.	☐	☐
5. When people feel they are being judged or controlled, they may become defensive, blocking communication.	☐	☐
6. Always listen attentively and let the other person finish what he or she is saying before you think of, or begin, your reply.	☐	☐
7. Be very careful of what you say around the company. That way, you won't upset anyone.	☐	☐
8. Being personal (being who you are), as opposed to playing a role (acting as a manager), helps the communication process.	☐	☐
9. If you are really clear about what you are saying, the other person is bound to understand.	☐	☐
10. Office memos are an ineffective way to communicate.	☐	☐

Chapter 4

Communicating

> *I*
> *know*
> *you believe*
> *you understand*
> *what you think*
> *I said*
> *but I'm not sure*
> *you realize*
> *that*
> *what you heard*
> *is not what I meant.*

Fritz Perls
In and Out of the Garbage Pail

Communications: A Matter of Perception

Communication problems are by far the most important issues we deal with in our consulting practices and in the classroom. Most of the time, they are brought to us under the guise of something else, like this one: "I'm the president of this company and he (the senior vice-president) just does whatever he pleases without checking with me. I'm going to make him fall into line, whatever the cost." And from the VP: "He's so buried in his sales activities that he (the president) doesn't know what's going on in the company. It's up to me to hold things together. That's my job." I've heard all kinds of labels applied to this common problem, but fundamentally the only thing that needs to get straightened out is better communications between them.

Or this one: "I go out and sell up a storm and those blankety-blank guys in production can't produce the stuff. They're ninety days past due on just about everything." That's the director of marketing speaking. Here's what the manufacturing manager is saying: "Those guys just write orders on anything they please. They make promises that make them look good, then they throw it over our fence and expect us to produce." Sales problem? Production problem? Neither — it's a communication problem. Both of these departments are excellent. They just haven't learned how to talk to each other and work out their mutual problems.

And so it goes, down to the lowest level in just about every company. Torrents of words in person, over the phone, in memos. Everybody believes that they are being understood because what they are saying is very clear to themselves. Well, most of the time they are not being understood, and this is why . . . .

Here are two people talking to each other: Francis is fifty-five years old. He grew up in a tough Irish-Catholic neighborhood in New York. He learned that if you want to survive, you must take a stand and not back down. In school he learned what the world is all about from a tightly controlled, conservative point of view. To Francis, things are either black or white, right or wrong. His way is right, and he knows it. This is his view of the world, and it surrounds him like an invisible bubble. Everything that he sees and hears — everyday conversation, TV shows, reading matter — goes through his invisible filter and is shaped to fit.

Art is forty-two. He grew up in a freewheeling part of San Francisco. His views of the world were shaped by Vietnam, smoking pot, permissive education, and parents who both worked. He sees the world in shades of gray. Everything that he sees and hears — people, radio, the newspaper, everyday conversation — goes through his invisible filter and is shaped to fit.

Art and Francis work together. When they start talking about things that concern their jobs, their filters are in full operation. Francis can only see Art's longish hair; every part of him just knows that, no matter what, this guy has got to be wrong. (This is not necessarily a conscious process. Filters can be not only invisible but unknown.) Art's filter only allows him to see a rigid, old-fashioned man who is over the hill. Oh, he plays at nice conversation, but can you imagine the outcome of anything these two try together? This type of mismatch is happening every day in every business in America. You wonder how any conversation can be productive. Too much of it isn't, which explains many of our business problems.

When you understand about differing perceptions (filters), you know how a police officer can get two diametrically opposing views of an accident from two eyewitnesses, how two people in an organization can have fundamentally different views of the company's purpose, and how two people can have a conversation and come away with totally different versions of what was said.

Learning to Speak

Words alone have no meaning. Only people can put meaning into words. Communication is a people process rather than a language process. If you want to become an effective communicator, you need to heighten your awareness of the human interaction involved. In addition to perception, there are two other aspects of communication that you need to understand. One is assumptions and the other is feelings.

Just as we assume that our messages are clearly received, so we assume that because something is important to us, it's important to another. We assume that our leadership is accepted, that everyone is looking at the problem the same way, or that our perception of reality is the only one. The problem with assumptions is that we rarely test them. In time they become, in our minds, concrete facts. A first step in good communications is to stop assuming that the other person understands what you are saying simply because you understand.

"Just stick with the facts and don't get emotional." Have you heard that one? Probably every day, in one way or another. It's generally accepted in American industry that feelings have no place. All we want is calm, pure logic. We weigh all our communications against the evidence (as we see it). If I put out the facts (after all, I know they are facts), then you ought to be able to understand my logic. Right? Wrong! The reality is that all of us are involved with our feelings all the time. Any time you believe you are dealing with another person based on facts, you are dealing with only half the issue. The other half is feelings. The antidote to poisonous assumptions is to test them by asking the other person how he or she sees the issue. That's an easy way to take care of the problem. The way to handle feelings is to acknowledge them and deal with them instead of pretending that they aren't there. That's a little tougher. Most of us have been pushing our feelings down for so long that we find it hard to identify or acknowledge them. For the moment, just add this to your awareness. We'll be dealing with feelings in many ways throughout the book.

Another cause of blocked communications is defensiveness on the listener's part. You have seen this happen often. A boss says something to a subordinate about work; a wife admonishes her husband; a parent tries to correct a child — and a stunned look comes over the recipient's face. Listeners may get angry, become supercalm, throw up their hands and walk away, get anxious, shout back, or display any of a dozen other such reactions. The result is that the words go unheard or at least unacknowledged. Then the speaker wonders, "What made that person so defensive?" Sometimes the speaker's presentation may cause you to defend yourself.

Here are some causes of defensive communications:

- The listener perceives the speaker's expression, tone of voice, manner of speech, or content as criticism or judgment.
- The listener perceives the communication as an attempt at control.
- The listener perceives strategies as manipulative, game-playing, or withholding information — not playing straight.
- The speaker shows no concern for the welfare of the other person.
- The speaker maintains poker-faced neutrality—playing a role, rather than being a person.
- An attitude of superiority, anything that makes the listener feel inadequate, nearly always creates a problem.
- Certainty, knowing it all or being really smart, raises the listener's hackles immediately and sets up a defensive posture.

Add to your awareness some thoughts on body language. All of the meaning in a conversation is not necessarily in the words. At one meeting, a member turned to another and asked, "Sam, I have the feeling that you're angry about something." "Who, me?" said Sam. "I'm not angry. Why should I be angry?" At the same time, his right fist methodically pounded the table, his face was red, and the veins stood out on his neck. Listening to Sam's words alone would have provided totally wrong clues to his feelings.

If you sensitize yourself to other people's movements, you will pick up important clues that indicate all may not be as heard. However, becoming an accurate interpreter of what certain actions mean is difficult, if not impossible. You should never try to psych out people based on their body language. It's simply a good basis for opening up a discussion to get at real feelings.

Learning to Listen

The other side of being a good communicator is being a good listener. People rarely listen carefully to each other. Why? To begin with, the receiver can take in words much faster than the speaker can put them out. So the mind wanders, filling the spaces between the words by taking a quick mental trip to the golf course, thinking about yesterday's meal, choosing a new car. Sometimes the side trip is so interesting that the listener may not get back before missing a sentence or two. It happens to everyone and a great deal of conversation is missed.

Sometimes we half-listen because our mind is working on a reply. Just watch how often you formulate a response and perhaps actually begin to speak before the other person has finished. Since thinking of a reply and fully listening are mutually exclusive, we lose a great deal of what is said to us.

Here's another, more complex reason for not listening. If you are really set in your view of the world, then truly listening to what another says means that you may have to change. You may not want to listen, because you dare not acknowledge what is being said. Truly listening implies a willingness to accept another view.

If you couple speaking problems with listening problems, you get some idea of the magnitude of the communications gap that exists among people in an organizational setting. With a slight applications twist you can also use your new knowledge to understand the etiology of the horrendous divorce rate in the United States, or why kids leave home and stop talking to their parents. If you would like to straighten out the problems of the world, improve the quality of life in your organization, or simply make your relationships more satisfying, practice being a good communicator.

Communicating Effectively

Communication is an interpersonal process. This means that becoming an effective communicator is not simply a matter of cleaning up your language; it's a question of improving the way you relate to people. It's a big job, but being a good communicator is an essential part of being a good manager (and a good husband, wife, lover, friend, father, mother, or member of the community). Because it requires patience, effort, and understanding, really effective managers (friends, husbands, wives) are rare. This is your chance to get a jump on the world.

Becoming Aware

Start your process by becoming and staying aware of the various dynamics in communications. Observe how you tune out someone who strikes you the wrong way because of dress, looks, ethnic background, or manner. Notice how little you hear of what this person says. Don't do anything about it, just observe.

Then notice how often you make judgments about others. Don't do anything about it, just notice what happens to your communication as a result.

Take careful note of the problems that are brought to you and think carefully about the nature of the problems. Do they involve technical issues or misunderstandings between individuals or groups? Just notice and think about it.

Check out all your assumptions when you make a decision or give instructions that affect other people. Write them down so you can see them clearly.

What kind of feelings have you had today? Anger, joy, relief, excitement, boredom? Try to notice each feeling as it comes up. What feelings did your actions arouse in others? Could you see anyone get angry? Excited? Notice.

Who became defensive when you spoke to them? How did they show it? By getting angry? Becoming supercalm? Turning pale? Walking away? Saying, "Yes, sir?"

Another aspect of awareness is a lot more complicated — awareness of who you really are. What constitutes your view of the world, what blocks and shields do you put up, and how do you project to others? Complete awareness is probably not possible, even with years of psychotherapy or study, but learning about yourself is important to the communication process.

The culture we grow up in has norms that establish our behavior. Each time we do something that's not a natural part of our own process, we superimpose a falseness over our real self. These layers build up over time, confusing our senses, until eventually we lose touch with our inner core and become a patchwork of "oughts" and "shoulds." Our self-perception gets off. Some of the messages we put out come from the superimposed layers, but once in a while a little of the "real us" comes through. Which is which? If we don't know, how are others to know?

The nearer we come to awareness of our core, the clearer our messages to others become. Communication with others at valuable levels of understanding becomes easier. Achieving this awareness requires a life-long process of introspection, being open to new inputs from others, working in small groups, or trying some well-person psychotherapy. How far you go with this is a matter of individual choice. Being aware of the possibilities is a good first step.

Awareness is a substantial part of learning. When you begin to understand your own actions and those of others, you automatically begin to make appropriate changes in your behavior to clear up your communication.

Being Congruent

Mean what you say and say what you mean. Learn to be direct without being demeaning or abusive. Concerns left unsaid always lead to assumptions on the part of others and this blocks communication. Anytime you leave a communication void, it gets filled with an "I assume."

People who speak with forked tongues create huge credibility gaps, so you must not only get it all out, but get it all out honestly. Straight talk is the death of interpersonal game-playing, which is an insidious and destructive form of human interaction.

Watch open, honest communication and the impact it has on others. Initially, people gasp because it is unusual to have everything up front. But once they settle down, they acknowledge their relief at being able to communicate honestly. Since they don't have to wonder, they feel less fatigue, which means they have more energy to invest in work and play.

One other discovery: If you become an open, honest communicator, others will. The only way to deal with someone who is open is to be open yourself. Axiom of the day: Openness and honesty beget openness and honesty. If only one or two in an organization start, the entire communication pattern of the organization begins to open up.

The Value of Straight Talk

Being able to say how you feel, admit your fears and weaknesses, and acknowledge your mistakes is a sign of great strength and a powerful communication device. Unfortunately, we learn that to admit a mistake is to show weakness, and any show of weakness is an improper managerial (or human) trait. These are myths perpetuated from the early days of riding tall in the saddle and from movies extolling the virtues of impassive gunmen. The John Wayne syndrome remains strong in the land and many managers wear it like a badge of honor. The problem is that the Old West is gone forever and in its place we have elbow-to-elbow people working at computers. Everything else is different, too, including aspirations. Maybe it's time to reconsider.

The manager who can say, "I don't know" or "Your idea sounds better than mine, let's try it" wins the hearts and trust of employees. The flag of honor can replace the red badge of courage, people can be who they are — somewhat imperfect. In an open environment, where people can be what they seem, trust is renewed and workers have twice as much energy for doing their jobs.

Being Personal

Most relationships in organizations are dictated by role. The boss speaks as the boss and is treated as such. People have titles on their doors, desks, and cards. Each one is a sign that says, "I want you to respect my position." Respect for the position is not the same as respect for the person. If I speak to your role, I am probably going to slant my statement, censor my feelings, and cover my tracks. If I speak to you as a person I respect, I am more likely to trust my instincts, express my feelings, tell you the whole story, take responsibility, and be who I am.

An excellent communicator exists in our local academic community, despite the fact it is a tightly controlled, high-fear/low-trust environment. Practically everything is done on a rigid hierarchy of rank, seniority, credentials, and snobbery. Everyone has multiple roles; one person may be professor, doctor, economist. The Academic Dean learned to get around that aspect of the system, while still living within it. He did so by being as fully human as possible.

He always moved away from his desk during an interview. He asked faculty members what they thought as well as telling them about his concerns. He never judged, sometimes coached, and was always interested in each individual, not just his agenda for the school. Faculty members, seldom conscious about his position, felt that a visit with him was rewarding. He was always personal. The communication always worked.

Office Memos

How many times in your career have you read an office memo and become angry about its contents? How many times has an office e-mail dampened your day? If you are an average worker, the answer is "often." Office memos and e-mails are a prime source of communication problems in organizations.

Memos are one-way and all such communication runs a high risk of being misunderstood, even when well-intentioned. But many memos are not well-intentioned; they are a means of hiding.

The good communicator prefers to communicate face-to-face whenever possible. One particularly blatant example: A lower-level manager, new to the company, feels put down by a supplier and dashes off a memo to the entire organization telling everyone not to deal with the offending company again. Recipients all down the line are angered. "Who is this guy passing out instructions?" "This company is a favorite of mine. I intend to continue with them." "There's always a wise ass in the company who thinks he owns the place." The damage done by that four-line memo will take months to repair. All of the recipients meet regularly every week. The manager could have presented the situation much better at a meeting and asked the group how to handle it.

Before writing a memo or sending an e-mail, think carefully of the reaction it will cause. Consider your reason for writing rather than saying it.

Listening for What Is Not Being Said

We often assume we know what the other person means. Sometimes we take in the actual words and let it go at that. "Well, Joan said it, so she must mean it." Not necessarily. What if you give me an assignment and I say, "Sure, boss." Is that the true reply? What if there's a little quiver in my voice, or a small drop of perspiration on my lip while I'm saying it? Maybe I'm saying okay because I'm afraid to tell you that I'm overloaded and this assignment will break my back. Have we communicated? Not unless you are noticing the incongruities — the slight twist of the head, the sharpness of the reply, the slouch of the shoulders, the too-rapid departure.

Earlier I talked about being aware, just noticing. When you have this down pat, move into action. If you have a doubt about the message, ask. Maybe you still won't get the true response, but maybe you will. Or, if you signal that you care when you ask the question, maybe you will get a straight answer the next time, or whenever you seem trustworthy enough. It's important to check out any incongruities and to let it be known that you're willing to discuss anything and everything. Eventually you will achieve the open communication you desire.

Being an Active Listener

To really hear what another person is saying, try this:

- Suspend judgment until all the information is in.
- Expect to learn something when someone speaks.
- Listen for intended meanings. Look behind the words and the way they are presented.
- Keep eye contact with the speaker.
- Use facial expressions such as nods and smiles to let the speaker know you are in contact.
- Take responsibility for understanding the content and feelings of the speaker. Respond in your own words to what you believe is the speaker's message. This gives the speaker an opportunity to acknowledge that this is what he or she meant, or to clean up the statement so that you get the real message being sent.

Sensitive Listening

An effective manager is a good coach. A coach never plays in the game and never tries to make the players adopt a specific style. As employees go through the learning process, the effective manager is encouraging and supportive. For the growing manager, becoming an effective listener satisfies many of the criteria for encouraging and supporting. Listening well is the most effective way to tell co-workers that you respect and care for them as persons.

To really hear what someone else is saying, you must see the world from that person's perspective. A Native American saying goes, "If you want to know a man you must walk a mile in his moccasins." When you enter other people's worlds, judgment is removed. You can see them or their problems in a new light. From this perspective you can get the feelings as well as the content of the message.

In a truly helping relationship (effective coaching), just being with people and letting them know you understand may be all the help needed to see the problem and its potential solution more clearly. This approach contrasts starkly with that of so-called "helpers" who freely give advice out of their views of the world, only to have the advice rejected and a communication blowup result.

Have you ever been asked to intervene in a lovers' quarrel and given the pair your best advice, only to have them get together and turn on you? A better and much more effective approach is to give up being helpful in the traditional sense and to become a sensitive listener, feeding back to the pair what you hear going on. When they really see clearly what's happening, they can fix things up themselves — a much more satisfying, permanent solution.

Whenever you are tempted to be a helper, to rush in and fix things, try the sensitive listening method instead. Get into the other person's world. You can do this by letting go of your bias and allowing yourself to hear. Then simply feed back to the other what you hear being said — not just the words, but the unsaid words, the feeling behind the spoken words. Do this in a relaxed, unhurried way and you will be a helper in the best sense of the word, allowing yourself to get a better picture of what's bothering the individual and enabling the person to find his or her own solution. Sensitive listening will turn out to be one of your most effective managerial tools.

Communications Checklist

Think back over all your communications during the past week, using this form as a guide. After you have completed the form, go over it and write down ways in which you could have been a more effective communicator.

1. When did you ask someone a question, putting that person on the spot, rather than stating your own feelings or beliefs?

2. How many times did you play "Yes, but ...."?

   • By discounting a proposal as being too expensive, too difficult, too late, too early, too ....

   • By discounting yourself because you're too tired, too old, too young, too dumb.

   • By saying, "Yes, but we tried that before and it didn't work."

- By giving someone a go-ahead on a project you knew wouldn't work so the person would deliberately be embarrassed.

3. Whom did you tune out because you don't agree with their views? How did you tune out?

4. How and when did you get defensive, blocking communication?

5. When did you lay a judgment on someone because you didn't like that person's looks, ideas, or ethnic background?

6. What happened at your meetings this week?

   - When did you formulate an answer before someone else finished speaking?

   - Which of your employees displayed a deaf ear? Why?

   - What conversation did you dominate?

   - What conversation did you not join? Why?

   - What new ideas did you reject out of hand?

   - When did you let your mind wander?

   - What games did you play — that is, when were you not playing straight?

   - When were you really certain, in no uncertain terms?

Additional Information

Books

How to Communicate Effectively and Handle Difficult People, Preston C. Ni, Burgess Publishing, 1999. Down to earth ideas that work.

The Positive Power of Praising People, Jerry Twentier, Contemporary Books, 1998. Based on the idea that praise is the least expensive and often most effective way of motivating others.

Communicating for Change, Roger D'Aprix, Jossey-Bass, 1996. How to use communications as a key element of management strategy.

Communicating Effectively: A Complete Guide for Better Managing, Susan Dellinger and Barbara Deane, Chilton Book Company, 1982. Just what the title says: a complete guide.

How to Manage Your Boss, Christopher Hegarty with Philip Goldberg, Rawson, Wade Publishers, 1980. The chapter on effective communications tells how to deal with your superior without setting up resentment.

Interpersonal Behavior, Anthony G. Athos and John J. Garbarro, Prentice-Hall, 1978. Two Harvard professors take you through their solutions to communications problems. One of the best books on the subject.

How to Interpret the Test for Chapter 4

If you answered "Yes" to number 3, you may be overlooking the real issue — feelings. "Let's not get emotional around here" blocks out the most important part of the communication.

A "Yes" to number 7 may indicate you are engaging in some verbal game-playing. Most people would rather have it straight, even if what you say upsets them.

The answer to number 9 is "No." Words don't have the same meaning to everyone. Each of our mental filters allows words to come through differently. This concept is explored in the chapter.

You may be surprised that the rest of the answers are "Yes." The reasons should become clear as you read through the chapter.

Chapter 5

A Motivation Checklist

What Do You Do About Motivation?

Take a quick run-through and mark each of these a "Yes" or "No." The answers are at the end of this chapter.

	Yes	No
1. Christmas bonuses keep people working hard all year long.	☐	☐
2. Having strict rules and enforcing them makes everyone appreciate a tight organization.	☐	☐
3. Salespeople usually do better when they are working for prizes in a contest.	☐	☐
4. The four-day work week is a real motivator.	☐	☐
5. Having employees punch a timecard ensures they will show up on time.	☐	☐
6. Threats of punishment for nonperformance are necessary for some people.	☐	☐
7. Company picnics or Christmas parties are always good for morale.	☐	☐
8. Giving gold stars for good behavior is one way of keeping children on track.	☐	☐
9. Special perks such as a good office and preferential parking build motivation.	☐	☐
10. Salary increases are motivators for everyone.	☐	☐

Chapter 5

Motivating

Intrinsic Versus Extrinsic Motivation

Management professionals agree substantially on the subject matter covered in the preceding chapters of this book. Collaborative teams have proven to be the most productive use of human resources, and good, clear communication is the foundation of a healthy business.

No such agreement exists on the subject of motivation. If you read through university texts on the subject, you will find theories galore: expectancy theory, reinforcement theory, need theory, need for achievement, job enrichment theory, and many more. Each theory has its proponents, body of research, and practitioners.

People have been trying to motivate others since the caveman took a club to his mate to encourage more speed out of her daily activities. Remnants of that motivational theory still exist in some of our organizations.

Today, the hot topic everywhere is productivity — the amount of work produced vs. the labor cost. Motivation becomes a key part of such discussions. How do we get people to produce more, to move faster, to think smarter, to perform better?

Most of the present theories have two principles in common:

- They are based on a system of rewards and punishments. The rewards may be as blatant as money or as subtle as peer recognition. The punishment may be loss of pay or loss of face. All are *extrinsic* to the person — they are applied by someone to someone else to make that person do something.

- There is always someone in charge of the process, a person or persons higher up in the hierarchy than those who need to be motivated.

The problem with all these systems is that they need constant effort to make them work; the moment the manager quits pushing or pulling, everything stops. The best example is sales management. The prevalent system runs constant contests (competition theory) to keep everyone on his or her toes. While the contest for the trip to Hawaii is going on, management is working on the next contest.

The negative aspects of this approach have been demonstrated over and over. People figure out ways to beat the game, and they come to expect the contest rewards as a regular part of their pay. The same with Christmas bonuses. They don't motivate much of anything, but cut them out and see how much trouble you get into.

Part of the problem is in how we define motivation. Frederick Herzberg did a good job when he defined everything we have been talking about so far as "movement." You charge someone's battery and he moves. Motivation, Herzberg says, is what happens when people charge their own batteries.[3] He means that motivation occurs from the inside — it's intrinsic.

Now this is very important, because I'm flip-flopping one of the most cherished concepts of many business owners and managers — the one that says, "If you want to get people motivated, kick them or bribe them." I'm saying that you can't motivate anyone. You can create movement if you want, but you'd better be prepared with some modern form of the old cattle prod, and you can't ever quit using it. You might also prepare yourself for some side effects such as resentment, apathy, hostility, even rebellion. You will need to become an expert in the adversary system. You might also lower your productivity sights, because, in the long run, you will never get more than average performance.

---

3. Frederick Herzberg, *Work and the Nature of Man* (New York: World, 1968).

Collaborating and Motivation

Giving people a piece of the action (participative management) is a critical aspect of intrinsic motivation. When people have an opportunity to collaborate with others in setting organizational goals, to join in making decisions, and to be involved in implementing group goals, the motivation is really powerful. Clearly, these things satisfy needs for growth and recognition. Besides creating a challenge, the company is saying, "I trust in you and I believe in you." When employees feel respected, barriers are removed, human energy is released, and people want to accomplish. Such internal power needs nothing from management. It is self-generating.

The Nature of the Job Itself

Automobile manufacturers found out about mindless work and its impact on the current generation of workers at Lordstown, where workers called constant local strikes, sabotaged cars, and generally made a mess out of what was supposed to be the most modern production facility of its time. Turning a bolt into place hundreds of times a day is hardly uplifting labor, particularly to the people of today. It was acceptable thirty years ago perhaps, but the world has changed.

Now the automakers have worker groups that get involved in work design. Along with the supervisors, production workers meet to discuss how specific jobs should be done, the speed of the assembly line, and movement of parts. They are involved in every aspect of their work. The Saturn Division of GM is designed for total worker participation. These conditions encourage camaraderie and joint effort. As a result, we are getting American cars with the quality buyers want.

The same is true in many companies in tune with the times. They are designing jobs with people's internal chargers in mind. If workers can't get excited about a job, you can't expect them to be motivated — and you can do absolutely nothing about it. (Of course, you can get temporary movement, but you will need to become an expert with a prod.)

Supporting the Winner Concept

All people are born to win and we come into life thinking of ourselves as winners. Many of us are changed into thinking of ourselves as losers through what we are told by significant people in our lives or by how these people behave toward us. Parents who withhold love as a form of punishment, teachers who use red pencils exclusively, clergy who promise only damnation, and bosses who criticize but never praise all encourage us to see ourselves as losers.

Only people who see themselves as winners are willing to take on new challenges, take risks, work hard, become leaders. Those who see themselves as losers keep a low profile, take a conservative approach to tasks and relationships, prefer the mainstream, relate poorly.

Clearly, winner concepts foster motivated behavior. The problem is, most managerial styles foster loser concepts and resultant demotivated behavior.

An effective manager who wants a highly motivated team is always supportive, never negative, always praises when it's deserved, criticizes behavior but never the person, expresses human feelings rather than value judgments, is honest and prizes honesty in others, and has an open-door policy that goes all the way to the heart.

The winner concept is nurtured by continual reinforcement of an individual's worth. Usually this is fostered in close-knit families. When we are in need of a fresh shot of confidence, most of us look to our family, and the close loved ones who really care. A wise manager interested in motivation fosters the family feeling in his or her organization. A family-like workplace where everyone is interested in and helps everyone else is more likely to produce winners than a sterile organization that goes by the book.

Having High Expectations

Managers with high expectations usually have high-performing employees. People like to reach high and perform well. Employees involved in goal setting often set higher standards than management would set for them.

An important aspect of goal setting, discussed more fully in Chapter 7, is to keep goals within reach. Setting them just out of reach does not cause stretching, it causes frustration and it is demotivating. At least seventy percent of your employees should be regularly achieving their goals.

A substantial amount of research has been done on self-fulfilling prophecies. Managers who believe their employees are highly-motivated people with great potential usually get good results. Managers who believe their employees are low performers usually wind up with the low performers.

We don't know exactly how this happens, but the results are well documented. It probably has to do with the same issue of self-worth. When people sense that they are valued, their internal motors rev up and they produce more.

Having a positive attitude about the abilities of your employees is more a state of the heart than a state of the art. It's less likely to be learned as a technique than it is to be an integral part of a positive approach to life.

Helping People Rekindle Their Own Burners

The first act in managing motivated people is to click in a new framework for thinking. We usually think of motivation as something the manager does to or for an employee to get the employee going. In the new context, motivation is an internal process that each person is born with and always possesses. Depending on how an individual has been treated during life, his or her motivation may be running on full power or may be buried under many layers of learned responses.

Parents start the extrinsic movement process by rewarding good behavior with treats, special occasions, or gold stars. Teachers continue the process with honor rewards, punishment, and grades. Businesses add to the dependence on an extrinsic system through competitive awards, bonuses, and special treatment. Eventually, the person comes to depend almost totally on external stimulation for motivation.

Once you understand this, you will want to stop lighting fires under people. Instead, help them rekindle their own burners. You must also recognize that the changeover may take some time. Many adults, suddenly called upon to take charge of their own directions and powers, find themselves temporarily immobilized. The external prods have stopped and the internal system is atrophied. Just as it takes physical therapy to rejuvenate injured or unused muscles, so it takes gentle, regular care to restart internal motivational generators.

Generally, the changeover process can be speeded along through understanding and good communication. When faced with a request for explicit directions about how to do a job, you can try to get people to examine alternative ways they might choose to do it. This is an important juncture because it simultaneously offers empowerment to employees and raises their worst fears that you are going to abandon them. Careful nurturing, along with a firm refusal to take responsibility, will encourage them to work the problem out themselves. In this way you remove yourself from the role of external battery charger, replacing that role with employees who have the beginnings of internal motivation.

This is a critical stage for most managers who are changing their style from authoritarian to participative. There's that trying period when people wonder what to do, get frustrated and often angry. Sometimes they see the manager as being lazy, uninterested, or as abdicating responsibilities. Faced with hostile attitudes and a slow-down in the work pace, many managers return to their old style.

If you are a true believer, you will stand your ground. The reward will be a workforce full of enthusiastic self-starters who require little in the way of supervision. Once you get real motivation on line, you will be able to take on the more important managerial task of being innovative. Managers stuck in the old model — checking time cards, telling people what to do and how to do it — have little time to be creative or to plan for the future of the organization.

If the locus of motivation is internal to the person, what can you, as a manager, do to help the changeover process along? In broad terms, two things:

1. You can get involved in improving the design of the job, which will enable your people's internal chargers to function.
2. You can become a special kind of leader — a caring, nurturing person in the style advocated throughout this book.

You may have some jobs that are just plain dull, that are simple, repetitive, and require little brainpower. How can you handle these jobs so they are performed with maximum efficiency? If at all possible, automate them out. This is the best answer in the long run.

Start by seeing whether you can get more autonomy into the job. Enrich it by upgrading the skills needed to do it. For the best ideas about how to do this, ask the people on the job. If you are someone they can trust, they will give you the ideas you need.

Finally, if you can't make the job more interesting and if automation is not in the picture, think about your hiring practices. Usually we try to hire "the best person" no matter what. The result is often overqualified people in dull jobs. This mismatch between the ability of people and their jobs is ubiquitous in American industry. Thousands of people with degrees are doing jobs that are unchallenging, essentially unmotivating. If you must find someone for a dull job, tell your candidate exactly what the job entails, and try to pick someone who will be satisfied doing that kind of work.

Redirecting Power

Most managers understand power as a force to be used externally, to be directed at another person or group. This power is used to reshape the environment, to make it match their view of how the world ought to be. Commonly, we shape our children so they will grow up the right way — our way. In relationships we often try to make over the other person. We try to dominate our wives and husbands. In friendships we enter arguments with the need to win. We want to make others change their views to match our own.

Similarly, the pull and tug between management and employees is a constant fact of organizational life. All the energy that goes into this struggle is unavailable to do the company's work. Such dissipation of energy affects both sides.

The formula for management success today is to transfer the traditional power exercised by those in command to power widely disseminated throughout the ranks. Empowerment begins with top management empowering those in the tier below, with power trickling on down throughout the organization. You will know you have succeeded when your people feel and say, "We did it ourselves."

What Do People Want from Their Jobs?

A Group Exercise for Managers

Objective: To give participants an opportunity to discuss what factors motivate employees.

Procedure: Distribute copies of the form, What Do People Want From Their Jobs? at the end of this chapter. Divide the group into subgroups of three to five people each.

1. Each individual, working alone, is to rank how he or she thinks employees would prioritize this list. Rank the most important factor as #1, the next most important factor #2, and so on. Enter your ranking in the column headed "Individual."

2. Take an average of the group's rating on each of the items and enter the results in the column headed "Group."

3. This same scale has been given to thousands of supervisors and managers around the country. They guessed that the employees would rank the factors this way:

    1. High wages
    2. Job security
    3. Promotion within the company
    4. Good working conditions
    5. Interesting work
    6. Personal loyalty of supervisor
    7. Tactful discipline
    8. Full appreciation of work done
    9. Help on personal problems
    10. Feeling of being in on things

    Enter these scores in the column headed Supervisors.

4. When thousands of employees were given the same exercise and asked what affects their morale most, their answers tend to follow this pattern.

    1. Full appreciation of work done
    2. Feeling of being in on things
    3. Help on personal problems
    4. Job security
    5. High wages
    6. Interesting work
    7. Promotion within the company
    8. Personal loyalty of supervisor
    9. Good working conditions
    10. Tactful discipline

    Enter these scores in the column headed Employees.

Note that the three items ranked at the top of the list by employees are the same three ranked by supervisors at the bottom of the list.

Discussion Questions

1. Compare your group's ratings with the ratings in the "Employees" column. How do they differ? What factors might account for the differences?

2. Why do you suppose the supervisors' ratings are so different from those of their employees?

3. If this form were to be used in your business (department) how similar would the results be?

4. What are the implications for rethinking what motivates people in your organization?

A Motivation Checklist

Use this list to check on your progress as you move from external to internal motivation in your business.

1. I understand the intrinsic nature of motivation. But I also acknowledge differences in my people. For some, holding out a carrot works; for others, it doesn't.

2. When someone does a good job, I make sure to give praise and provide commensurate rewards.

3. If I hand out any bonuses, I do it on a team basis.

4. I don't put highly qualified people in dull jobs.

5. I scrutinize jobs continuously to see how they can be made more autonomous and how I can give more responsibility.

6. Providing opportunities for individual growth is an important part of my strategic plan.

7. I get commitment to goals by letting everyone participate in their formulation.

8. I value and nurture intrapreneurship (being an entrepreneur within the organization).

9. I am systematically reducing the number of rules under which we work.

10. Low-stress working conditions are a focus of our planning.

Additional Information

Books

Ten Minute Guide to Motivating People, Nancy Stevenson, MacMillan Publishing Co., 2000. Basic strategies for getting people to achieve goals.

Stop Whining and Start Winning, Frank Pacetta, Harper Business, 2000. A call for leaders to get off their butts and free up their workforces.

Empowerment Takes More Than a Minute, Ken Blanchard, Berrett-Koehler, 1999. Explains the concrete steps managers can take to fully empower their employees. Includes sharing information and developing teams.

Motivating People, Dayle M. Smith, Barrons Educational Series, 1977. Methods for communicating enthusiasm to employees.

75 Best Business Practices for Socially Responsible Companies, Alan Reder, Tarcher Putnam, 1995. How ethically motivated companies integrate successful practices into the workplace.

Intrinsic Motivation, Edward L. Deci, Plenum Press, 1975. This is heavy reading, but if you are curious about the nature and importance of the subject, give it a try.

Work and the Nature of Man, Frederick Herzberg, World, 1968. Classic work on motivation.

Motivation and Productivity, Saul W. Gellerman, Amacom, 1963. This is the basic book on the subject and provides the historical background of current concepts.

Resources

Every book written on the subject of human behavior in organizations has something to say about motivation. Just go to the business section in your library and start scanning.

How to Interpret the Test for Chapter 5

According to the best understanding we have of how people act, and if we have a common definition of motivation, the answer to all of these questions is "No," which may surprise you. Read Chapter 5 for a better understanding of why the old tricks don't work.

Chapter 6

Rate Yourself on Delegating

Test how well you delegate against the statements that follow. See the expert's answers at the end of this chapter.

	Yes	No
1. Being in control at all times is important.	☐	☐
2. My employees can't handle assignments unless I watch them.	☐	☐
3. I am the only one who can do it right.	☐	☐
4. I know what's going on around here all the time.	☐	☐
5. Getting properly trained is the responsibility of the individual employee.	☐	☐
6. I have so much work I often stay late or take work home.	☐	☐
7. I have several long-range projects waiting for some free time so I can start on them.	☐	☐
8. My employees come to me regularly for advice and instruction.	☐	☐
9. I have a reputation as a real problem-solver, so when problems get sticky my employees bring them to me.	☐	☐
10. My people know I am available to help and they sometimes call me at home.	☐	☐
11. I give very precise instructions about how things should be done.	☐	☐
12. I believe the less people know about the inside of the business, the less trouble they get into.	☐	☐

Chapter 6

Delegating

The Value of Delegation

Delegation is the process of assigning a project or activity and sharing the responsibility for its outcome. It may be the most important skill a manager can develop. The mastery of this crucial skill spells the difference between being a manager, someone who gets things accomplished through people, and an administrator, someone who accomplishes their goals by moving paper. There are three basic reasons why mastering the art of delegation is important to your success as a manager.

- Delegation allows you to perform your job better. It is the key that allows you to spend more time managing and less time on repetitive, nonessential tasks.

- Delegation prepares you to be delegated to, preparing you for greater responsibility and higher levels of experience.

- Delegation trains others for the opportunity to move into your job when you are absent temporarily, on vacation, or for other reasons, and when you are ready to move up or out.

Preparing for Delegation

There are two sides to the delegation preparation process. A manager must be prepared to let go of the need to implement the actual project itself, and the subordinate(s) must be prepared to accept it. Let's face it, no one can do your job as well as you can, particularly if they aren't trained to do so. As a result, many managers fail to take the time to develop a strategy for effectively delegating tasks and projects. We want to emphasize that delegation is not simply asking somebody to perform an activity to help you finish your project. Certainly, there are times when you will ask someone else to copy a document or make a telephone call for you, or even perform tasks of a delicate and complicated nature. But true delegation requires that you actually give over the responsibility for the whole task or project, along with the necessary authority to get it done. Here are a few of the symptoms that may indicate to you the need to sharpen your delegation skills:

- Working most nights and weekends — no time for yourself. Sometimes it is helpful to look into exactly why you are in this predicament. It is not unheard of for some managers to use their heavy workload as a way to avoid being places they'd rather not be or to avoid doing things they'd rather not do. When that's the case, not delegating may appear to be the better solution. But remember, the stressors that build up when using work as an escape hatch can be hazardous to your health! If, after examining the facts, you don't seem to fit into this category, then delegation is your way out.

- Not enough time to return telephone calls and e-mail. Somehow, most of us seem to be able to return the messages we want or have to. Not responding to others creates a barrier that can inhibit your ability to be recognized or promoted for your good work. Block out a period of time on your daily calendar that is exclusively for returning messages and use it.

- No time to see people on business matters. Block out time in your calendar every day for appointments with others. Delegate to someone else the responsibility for filling that block of time.

- Missing deadlines. This can be dangerous to your organizational future, and in some cases can be a career killer. Unless you are really self-destructive, you'll want to do anything to avoid this. Learning to delegate properly is an easy solution.

- Doing the job you got promoted from. Many managers feel that since they were promoted for doing a good job in their previous position, they must continue doing the work they got recognized for. If you get promoted to a position that oversees what you previously did, your first task is to properly train a replacement. If you don't have a replacement, then you haven't really been promoted. You have simply been given more responsibility.

- No time to plan. First and foremost, planning requires the ability to decide what is important—in other words, the ability to prioritize. The more you have to do, the higher the probability that you will focus your attention on just putting out the next fire. As a manager you need to create a broader horizon for yourself than that. Delegating can create windows of time that you can use to plan the direction that you and your group are heading.

You'll notice that almost all of these symptoms involve time. That is why delegation is so crucial for good management; it creates time for you to do what you are (or should be) getting paid for, managing people. But your willingness to let go of some of the work is only half the story.

Employees cannot be expected to take responsibility for work they have not been trained to do. An effective manager of people starts out early by selecting people who are willing to be trained to take more responsibility. Start by looking for specific traits, such as those listed below — especially important are willingness and self-discipline.

- Willingness
- Self-discipline
- Plan their own work
- Help others plan
- Leadership
- Follow-through
- Self-confidence
- Initiative
- Loyalty
- Ambition

Training is done by first giving small amounts of responsibility to a worker or team of workers, monitoring their progress, and making corrections where necessary. In some situations, redistributing your group's work assignments may go hand in hand with selecting the proper people with whom to begin the delegation process.

First do a study of the group's workload as a whole. The idea is to find out how work is now allocated, how much of it is necessary, who should do it if it is necessary, and how much time is available to do new, developmental tasks. It's a good idea to involve the group in this process by having them meet together with you to create a work-flow diagram, and for each member to assess the time it takes for him or her to do their portion. Let the group decide how to reallocate work so that the unit can run more efficiently, if that is necessary. For this to be effective, there needs to be a prior atmosphere of trust established (see Chapter 3, Team Building). Otherwise, workers may not be honest about the amount of work they do or the amount of time available for them to do other things.

Delegate Duties for Training

It has been shown that seventy-five percent of employees want more responsibility. It is important, however, that this increased responsibility leads to something for them. New assignments, then, should encompass as much skill development as possible. The following are some criteria for selecting duties that could be beneficial for employee development:

- Delegate assignments that an employee needs to strengthen special weaknesses. Nobody is likely to have just the right mix of skills to do a delegated assignment exactly to your liking. By selecting the proper assignment to delegate, you can help a subordinate correct weaknesses and develop compensatory skills.

- Delegate a variety of duties to test your employee's versatility and add interest to his or her job. Variety in a job makes it more interesting. However, too many and too diverse details can overburden and kill interest altogether, so add spice carefully.

- Delegate duties that could lead directly to promotion. Everyone performs better when they know their performance may lead to better things.

Three-Stage Delegating

The usual method of delegating is the sink-or-swim method. "Here's the job. Let's see if you can handle it." The odds are you will get a sinker. A better method is to be a coach. Coaching managers are the best and rarest kind. Coaches neither run onto the field to take over the job nor do they leave the players to their own devices. They offer expertise, new methods, continual training, support, and pep talks. They want everyone to be a winner. They get their satisfaction from putting the team together and standing behind it. Plan your delegating just as you would any other important training function of the company. Use the act of delegating to prepare team members to take on added responsibility. When the goals and the ways to reach them have been agreed upon, step aside and wait for the first report.

Not everyone is ready to take on a fully delegated task. Classify your people into these three categories and delegate accordingly.

1. Hand-holding. New or untried people in your organization don't want to be thrown to the wolves, and you would probably be uncomfortable letting them go unsupervised on a newly delegated task. For a time, until you are both comfortable, be a partner in the task, participating in the decisions, checking along the way. Do this in your best participative style, remembering that the purpose of this relationship is to train members of the group to carry the ball on their own.

2. Consulting. When you and they both feel ready, let them go off on their own. Let them feel free to come to you whenever they want help and information. Use your best coaching techniques, but remain outside the project, only responding when called upon. This gives your people the feeling of being supported without constricting their style.

3. Hands-off. This is for employees who feel confident in their abilities and whom you really trust to do the job right. Delegate the total project and step aside. This is your chance to get back to more creative work. Wait for results. Last, and by no means least, praise! Whenever you can, find a reason to be supportive and do it in a clear way. Telling employees they are doing a good job is one of the most important things you can do. Many managers find this difficult; others forget to do it. The most common complaint from employees is, "My boss doesn't acknowledge when I do a good job." Nothing gets results faster than honest praise. Practice it regularly.

More Delegating Tips

If you have prepared yourself and your employees properly, actually delegating the work is fairly simple. Select an activity or project that meets one or more of the criteria discussed earlier. Again, it is important that the assignment is one that the employee can learn from. Then follow these steps:

- Prepare a written synopsis of the assignment. This document, perhaps in an amended version, will be the record of what you and your employee agree to be the scope of the delegated assignment and the deadlines required.

- Go to a neutral place. A conference room or some other place that is not the territory of either of you seems to work the best when discussing the delegation of an assignment.

- Determine willingness to take a new assignment. If an employee feels that this assignment is being forced upon them, rather than of mutual benefit, the quality of the work and the speed at which it is accomplished will suffer. Describe the new assignment in terms of their benefits, as discussed above.

- Explain the job thoroughly. Bring in others who may have experience with the tasks involved, to help if necessary. Be sure to create an environment where questions are encouraged.

- Give them the synopsis to study. It is important that the employee has time to review the project on his or her own time. Questions about processes, deadlines, and expectations often take some time to surface.

- Agree to meet again for final clarification and a preliminary handoff. Be ready to answer any and all questions to your mutual satisfaction. Go over any areas of confusion or ambiguity. Finally, ask the employee to describe to you in his or her own words the full scope of what their assignment is, and what steps they will take to accomplish it. Finally, set a date and time for your first progress meeting.

Keep It Delegated!

One of the most common reasons the delegation process fails is that the manager takes the work back. This must be avoided at all costs. Once you take back one delegated assignment, all of them will end up back on your desk. Here are some of the reasons managers take back delegated work.

- The scope of the project was not properly outlined. Don't hand off an assignment until you are sure that all the employee's questions have been answered. The better you planned and prepared your briefing, of course, the fewer but more precise questions you will get.

- The employee loses confidence in his or her ability to do the assignment. This may be the case if this is the first time that your delegatees have been asked to take responsibility and work on their own. Remember, it is your job to be supportive and available if you want delegation to work. Hand-holding is critical here. Sincere praise can work wonders in these situations as well.

- The manager didn't really delegate the project. You must be sure that your subordinates feel that this project belongs to them. Encourage them to search for solutions to the problems that inevitably come up, and be available to answer questions. They should be aware that the responsibility for the assignment's completion belongs to them.

- The assignment went to the wrong person. Occasionally you can make a mistake in matching people to projects. Rather than taking it back, assign it to somebody else and prepare another, more suitable assignment for the person for whom it was a mismatch. If you have prepared well, this will rarely happen.

The Last Step

The process of delegation accomplishes two tasks that are essential to becoming a better manager. The first is that it clears your desk for more managerial and fewer clerical or routine tasks. Second, it creates an opportunity for you to interact with your employees on a less structured and routine basis, opening the door for more motivational interactions and training. Needless to say, then, there is no effective delegation without proper followup. You will need to evaluate the improvement in your skills as a delegator on an ongoing basis.

The following four questions can help you stay on track:

1. Have I delegated enough? If you are still devoting a significant portion of your day to writing reports and filling out forms, the answer here is probably "no."

2. Have I delegated too much? If others are making decisions that your boss expects you to be making, the answer may be "yes." Rather than taking back the assignment, try talking this over with your boss. Perhaps they need to be delegating some of their work to you!

3. Have I delegated to the right people? Not all of your choices are going to work the first time. Try shifting assignments around. Remember, twenty-five percent of people simply aren't interested in increased responsibility.

4. Have I really delegated? If you've confined your role in the process to being an advisor or coach, if you are getting timely reports from your employees, and if the work is being completed on time, then you are delegating.

It will take a while for your employees to get used to this new way of doing things, so you may be more involved than you like as you get things off the ground. Be patient; you'll be astonished at how quickly employees catch on to a new assignment if you have prepared them for it, and how much more smooth and pleasurable your own job becomes.

Additional Information

Books

Effective Delegation, Chris Roebuck, Amacom, 1999. Getting your team to work more effectively as you delegate responsibility to them.

Thriving on Chaos, Tom Peters, Knopf, 1987. In chapter L-7, Peters calls delegation the "*sine qua non* of empowerment," then explains why.

The Art and Skill of Delegation, Lawrence Steinmetz, Addison-Wesley, 1976. Good basic background.

No Nonsense Delegation, Dale D. McConkey, Amacom, 1974. How-to, for a hands-on approach.

How to Interpret the Test for Chapter 6

If you answered "Yes" to more than two of these questions, you may not be managing as effectively as you could be. The information in Chapter 6 will give you important new perspectives on the importance of delegating.

Chapter 7

What Is Your G-S Quotient?

Test your G-S (goal setting) style against the statements below, then see the last page of this chapter for comments.

	Yes	No
1. I work against a comprehensive business plan or a formal long-range strategic plan.	☐	☐
2. My company (group) has an organizational plan that is revised annually.	☐	☐
3. All my employees have individual plans that cover their goals for the year.	☐	☐
4. I meet with my employees regularly to review their progress toward their goals.	☐	☐
5. I meet with my team regularly to check goal progress.	☐	☐
6. When a goal is set, I make sure it is monitored and doesn't fall through the cracks.	☐	☐
7. I build my relationships with subordinates around tasks we mutually identify and pursue.	☐	☐
8. I feel good when I relinquish control and pass responsibility on to others.	☐	☐
9. Company goals are set by all the key people, not just by me.	☐	☐
10. I praise my employees freely when they accomplish their goals.	☐	☐

Chapter 7

Goal Setting

The Benefits of Goal Setting

"What do I expect this person to do?"

"What does the company expect of me?"

When managers and their subordinates can answer these questions completely and explicitly, they have come a long way toward solving both the operational and interpersonal problems of the organization.

Effective management consists of striking a balance between task and relationship, between activities and people. Many managers tune out the behavioral scientists' continual emphasis on people issues, others accept them in theory but don't really put them into practice. Especially for entrepreneurs, amorphous issues like collaboration, motivation, and even stress management don't have the impact that fits an action-oriented style. Goal setting does.

Goal setting has all these advantages:

- It helps guard against chin-down management, the kind where you can only see a foot in front of you. Constantly running around stamping out crises consumes a lot of energy, keeps the staff confused, and never allows you to plan. Planning is a good way to prevent a crisis.

- Having goals, even short-term goals, brings the organization together, all headed in one direction.
- Setting goals for individual employees gives them activities they can pursue on their own.
- When individuals have set goals, they can fulfill their needs for autonomy and challenge, two highly sought-after aspects of a rewarding job.
- Goals give management a concrete way to measure performance.
- Goal setting is a collaborative effort — manager and subordinates work together to set goals that meet the organization's objectives. Teams of people working together toward mutually acceptable goals is a most satisfying human endeavor.

Managing with specific goals produces commitment and profits when goal setting is interactive. The effort must be mutual. In every documented case of failure of a goal-oriented program, collaboration was missing; the goals had been set by management without including in the process the people who were to carry out the task.

Goal setting works best when it is part of a strategic plan. Such plans usually set long-term objectives for the entire organization. Then short-term departmental goals are set, followed by each manager working out goals with individual employees, all geared toward jointly achieving the organization's and employee's goals.

For the smaller company, the original business plan sets out objectives for the first few years, paving the way for setting operational (short-term) goals. In very small firms, the principals should sit down together and commit to writing where the company is going, describing the business as they see it and how it should evolve.

The Form and Style of Goal Setting

The two kinds of goal setting are: (1) Organizational goal setting, which states objectives for a company, unit, or work team. This is usually done in a series of group meetings; (2) Individual goal setting, which is done by the employee and manager. The same principles apply to both.

- Setting goals for everything is unwieldy and produces a paperwork explosion. Usually, about twenty percent of the work to be done is important enough to warrant setting specific goals. The balance of the work is usually routine or part of clearly understood processes and duties.

- Goals should be stated concisely. If you need more than one sheet of paper to write out a complete goal, cut the goal down to size.

- Goals must be specific. Many statements that pass for goals are too general. A good example: "Our aim is to increase profits." Action is not specified. A better goal would be "We will increase profits by ten percent between April 1 and October 31." Then the balance of the statement could spell out how it will be done.

- Goals must be measurable. Some people goals are behaviorally oriented — for example, to upgrade an educational deficiency — but you need some clear way to recognize the goal has been reached.

- Each goal must be accompanied by an action plan. How are we going to get from here to there?

- Goals must be realistic — you should be able to achieve the goal within the time specified. Goal setting can be a destructive process if objectives are always set just out of reach.

- Goals must have value to the company and must be intrinsically rewarding to the people who carry them out. A goal should be important to everyone. This is a good reason not to set goals for routine matters.

The sequence of activity in goal setting is:

1. State the problem as best you can.
2. Decide what you want to accomplish.
3. State the end result — the goal you will have achieved once you have solved the problem.
4. Set down the possible actions you might take, including the measurements you will use. Tell how you will know when you have achieved the goal.
5. Refine the possibilities into a clear, concrete action plan.

A good, clear goal-setting program gives everyone a target to work toward. It gives you checkpoints to see if you are accomplishing your company objectives and it gets everyone working at their creative best.

Resistance to Setting Goals

It is no secret that setting goals can often be a lot easier than reaching them. Unanticipated events, inadequate information, and too little planning are ever-present challenges that managers must be prepared to face. We know that reaching personal and organizational goals requires careful planning. But often, despite the best-laid plans and regardless of how clear the path to a goal may seem, things can get in the way of achieving it. In this regard, it often helps to look at any hidden resistance you or others may have to achieving set goals. Once this resistance is clearly identified, steps can be taken to overcome it. Often, merely identifying a resistance is enough to start the process of reducing its influence. In the final analysis, resistance mostly arises due to a negative belief regarding the value of the goal in question. It is, therefore, important for a manager to get all resistance out in the open and assess the potential impact. A good strategic plan includes ways to overcome or work around as many forms of resistance as possible.

The accomplishment of goals always creates change of some sort. Change creates anxiety, however, even when the change is perceived as being a good one. When anxiety is present in an individual or group, resistance to change is inevitable.

Resistance can be divided into two basic categories which need to be approached in different ways. The first type of resistance is organizational. This springs from the way the organization itself is structured. In most organizations, the "not invented here" resistance is often the most common impediment. It is common knowledge that setting goals without getting the cooperation of those responsible for reaching them is looking for trouble. But it is amazing how often this is overlooked in the goal-setting process.

Even if a department or group sets its own goals, there can be resistance to them. A goal may be perceived as being in conflict with other goals. Setting a goal of high customer satisfaction may conflict with another goal: limiting the time spent responding to customer complaints, for example.

In other cases, a goal may be seen as taking the group in a wrong direction. A department that takes pride in the quality of its output may resist a goal that requires producing a product using cheaper materials. This type of resistance is composed of the personal anxieties of those involved in the outcome. In other words, the accomplishment of certain goals may be perceived as threatening to the survival of something that an employee or a group of employees feel is important. Obviously, goals such as reducing the workforce by twenty percent or moving the company to another locality fit into this category, but so do things like changing styles of uniforms, altering work assignments, or perhaps even changing the company logo.

When goals are in conflict, resistance can occur because the new goal appears to be inconsistent with goals previously put forth and agreed upon. If the new goal is not really inconsistent, then a clear description of how the new goal fits with the mission and direction of the organization is in order. If the new goal is a departure from the old order, then it needs to be clearly stated as such. A discussion of what the new order will be and how the group needs to organize to respond to the change needs to be initiated. There should be opportunity given for group members to freely discuss any issues that arise as a result.

When the issues are of a more personal nature, anger and resentment may be present. If these are allowed to grow without an outlet for their healthy release, problems ranging from increased absenteeism to sabotage can result. Obviously, it is sometimes necessary to alter work assignments or lay people off. These actions often confuse and anger the people impacted by them. Where many organizations fail their employees is in avoiding discussing the need for such actions, perhaps in the hope that rumors and resentments will subside, allowing business as usual to once again prevail. That seldom happens.

Organizations that operate from a team-building concept have an outlet for dealing with negative outcomes and discussing difficult issues. In these organizations, time has been spent to build a level of trust between workers and management at all levels. When difficult times arise, resistance is minimized through open and honest communication about the thorny issues.

The Effective Goal-Setting Manager

Effective goal setting managers don't need to be in tight control. "I will let you know when I have the job finished, boss," followed by days of silence, is soothing to their ears. They don't think about what might be happening; they feel sure that the commendable job their subordinates are doing will add up to accomplishment of the organizational goals. What kind of people are our relaxed managers? How did they get everyone working without their direction? And what are they doing while others are doing the "work?"

- They trust themselves and their own ability, which is the first step to trusting others.
- They trust the competency of their people.
- They are positive individuals; they believe the job will get done properly and that people will work hard to see that it happens.
- Our managers are people developers. They pride themselves on what their people do, not on what they themselves do. They allow their people to do the job the way they see fit.
- They set high standards and expect people to achieve them.
- At the beginning of each year, they sit down with their people individually and together they work out plans for the year. Individual goals are set that feed into the company's master plan. Effective goal-setting managers strive for clarity, checking to make sure that they and their employees understand each other, that they are both using the same words to mean the same thing. This is a lengthy process; it takes many meetings over several weeks. But in the end, each person has a written plan for the year.
- During the year, from time to time, they meet with each person to discuss his or her progress. They ask the person to show clear evidence of what work is being done and the two of them review this together. If things are going well, the employee gets ample praise. If things are not going well, the manager offers new ideas and new approaches. Sometimes goals are adjusted or reset because they may have been set too high, or because circumstances have changed. The manager never allows anyone to flounder around until it's too late to make corrections.
- Periodically, effective goal-setting managers get the whole group together to discuss goals. In these open periods of exchange of information, goals are reexamined and reset both for the group and for its individual members. People are teamed on demanding projects.

If you, as a stranger, walked in on the managers' departments, your senses would tell you this is a smoothly functioning, human place. There is a fluidity, a whir of motion. There are no clanks or grinds of friction — nothing is jammed. Everyone who works here feels it too, which adds to the general level of excitement.

Effective goal setting is a simple procedure for an integrated manager. It flows out of total commitment to developing an autonomous workforce, and a sensitive awareness of one's own role in the process.

Goal Setting by Design

This is a team activity to establish a goal-setting procedure.

☐ Sift through all the major problems facing your organization and pick one that needs attention. Don't necessarily go for the most important one; pick one that you feel capable of handling. After you get the hang of goal setting, you can take on more difficult issues.

☐ State the problem in one sentence. This may sound difficult, but it's important that you work this through so you know you are dealing with the central issue. Example:

Problem: Overtime in the shop is running our costs way up.

☐ In one sentence, write the desired solution. Example:

Desired solution: Deliver the same output in regular hours.

You have now completed the first part of goal setting by defining the expected goal in general terms.

☐ Clean up the "desired solution" statement so it is concrete and specific, rather than general. As a goal statement it should also be readily verifiable — that is, you should be able to see and measure it.

After some discussion you might decide that reducing the overtime to zero all at once is not realistic, but that it could be reduced by fifty percent over a four-month period. The goal statement would then read:

Reduce the shop overtime from 240 hours per month to 120 hours per month, while maintaining the same level of shipments, by (month and year).

Now you have a clear goal that can be tracked and measured.

☐ List all the various actions you might take to reach the goal. Do this in a brainstorming session, getting out as many ideas as possible. Don't analyze them to see if they are feasible. Just get ideas going.

☐ Using the team consensus process (see Chapter 3), select the activities that will realistically attain the goal and that everyone involved can support.

☐ Assign a project leader to each action item. The project leader writes up a proposal for accomplishing the action item and presents the solution to the team for their approval.

☐ Assign each action item a start-up date and a completion date and make one person responsible.

☐ The team decides who is coordinator of the plan and makes that person responsible for monitoring progress toward completion of the goal.

☐ Decide on measuring devices. How will milestones be checked and the final results verified?

☐ Decide when progress reports are due and who will make them. Assign meeting dates for the team to monitor results.

☐ Write up the complete plan in as few words as possible. Give each member of the team a copy.

☐ Assuming that the members of the team are the people who will make the plan work, the criterion for having everyone on the work team involved has been satisfied. If other work teams must be involved, meetings should be held to explain the plan to them. They must all buy into the plan if it is to succeed. If changes are called for, the plan should be reworked by the initial team. Consensus on the final plan is essential so that everyone is committed to achieving the goal.

Additional Information

Books

Performance Management: Tapping Your Organization's People Potential, American Productivity Control Center, 1999. Explores how a well-executed performance management system can deliver articulated goals.

Successful Management by Objectives, Karl Albrecht, Prentice-Hall, 1978. Easy reading about how to turn "fuzzies" into real goals.

Effective Management by Objectives, W.J. Reddin, McGraw-Hill, 1971. The larger view by a well-known management consultant.

How to Interpret the Test for Chapter 7

A "Yes" to all ten statements puts you right at the top of management proficiency.

Chapter 8

How Do You Rate on Performance Appraisal?

Test your performance appraiser style by responding to these statements below. Interpretation of this test is at the end of this chapter.

	Yes	No
1. Whether I have two employees or two hundred, I have a formal, written, performance evaluation system.	☐	☐
2. I enjoy the appraisal process because it gives me a chance to work closely with my employees on their personal development.	☐	☐
3. I complete my evaluations on time and I insist that managers under me do reviews on a regular basis and complete them on time.	☐	☐
4. I do not use an appraisal form that judges people on traits such as aggressiveness, cooperation, or leadership ability.	☐	☐
5. I meet with my subordinates regularly throughout the year to talk about their performance and to help them improve.	☐	☐
6. I always praise people immediately when they do something well. I don't save it for the annual review.	☐	☐
7. When someone makes a mistake, I discuss it with him or her immediately, with the goal of continual improvement. I never shout, and I never punish mistakes.	☐	☐
8. I involve my subordinates in the review process by having them evaluate their own performance in writing before we meet.	☐	☐
9. I work with my subordinates to set measurable goals for the coming year. I use these goals as a basis for evaluating performance.	☐	☐
10. I ask subordinates to give me feedback on my performance and to suggest ways that we can work together better.	☐	☐

Chapter 8

Evaluating

Appraisal for What Purpose?

Probably the least understood aspect of human resources development is performance appraisal. Managers in large organizations routinely fill out annual employee evaluations. They do this to fulfill some general need to have data in a personnel file, or to justify a raise. Rarely does a manager see this as other than an unwanted chore. Yet performance appraisal embodies every element of good people management and offers a precise way to develop subordinates' abilities.

This is the key — performance appraisal works best when used as a tool to develop people. It does not work well when it is used by a manager to punish a disliked employee, to satisfy personnel record-keeping, to justify giving a raise, or to pigeonhole someone. Performance appraisal works best when used primarily as a vehicle for getting people together to talk about their work-related problems in an effort to develop skills.

Performance appraisal is not a burden to be avoided, as so many organizations do. Whether a company employs two people, two hundred, or two thousand, it needs to evaluate its employees in a fair way. Consider these important issues:

- Everybody wants feedback about how they are doing. It starts when we first learn to talk. "Mommy, am I good?" We want to know from those we look up to (in this case our parents) that we are acceptable, that our behavior is okay. If it's not okay, we want to know what the standards of acceptability are, so we can get the strokes, the caring that we need.

- In school we learn that report cards come out at specific times, and that the grades will tell us how we are measuring up to standards. We learn that good grades will get us into college and later into graduate school, and that along the way they will get us recognition. In the organizational environment we want this feedback too, but often it's omitted.

- Without accurate, timely performance appraisal you cannot differentiate high achievers from ordinary workers. This results in indiscriminate pay raises and sends out signals that superior work is not rewarded.

- Omitted or sloppy evaluations indicate a lack of communication. Subordinates don't know where they stand with their managers and often take refuge in silence. This wall between people reduces organizational effectiveness and results in lower productivity.

- One of a manager's most important jobs is to develop people. Development requires regular counseling sessions and evaluation of the work being done. Performance appraisal is a summary of these activities.

Constructive Criticism Produces Growth

Many managers take the approach that judging employees is improper — they have no right to risk hurting others' feelings by telling them what's wrong with their performance. The fearful manager who takes this attitude does a disservice to both the organization and his employee. We have seen managers who have spent years trying to keep the peace by continually giving positive evaluations — only to wind up with ineffective employees who believed they were doing well.

A case in point: A printing company had an order-entry and invoicing department headed by Millie, an employee of fifteen years. She had an abrasive way of handling her subordinates that caused much dissension and turnover.

Her superior, Bob, demanded good performance but he never set criteria or coached her. Typically, he would chew Millie out when things went wrong, but otherwise he let her run her department as she pleased.

At annual review time, Bob took the position that if he encouraged her with a raise, she would somehow shape up. He would write "Good" or "Excellent" on her form, give her a cursory compliment, increase her salary, and get her out of the office fast.

This went on for fifteen years. By then the company had grown so large that when management performance was finally discussed, Millie became the center of attention. If her management abilities could not be brought up to par, the entire company would suffer. It was time to tell Millie the truth.

Bob called her in and she was told that her management style had been ineffective all along and she would have to treat her employees better.

Can you put yourself in Millie's shoes? Imagine her feelings! Never having received any prior criticism, she assumed she was doing well. Now, after fifteen years of service, she had to reevaluate her entire work life.

At that point in the company's growth Bob had no alternative, yet his treatment of Millie wound up being cruel and inhuman. All of this could have been prevented if he had done honest evaluations and developed Millie's management style in a supportive way.

On the other side, how many employees leave a perfectly good job because no one ever recognizes their superior work? This too could be prevented with a simple personal acknowledgment and by putting into the records a formal evaluation that says, "I appreciate you."

Why Performance Appraisal Systems Fail

Performance appraisal has been around many companies for years with mixed results. When systems fail, one or more of these issues is involved:

- The company uses trait ratings. Managers are often asked to rate employees on such traits as judgment, aggressiveness, and leadership. Such systems are ineffective because they don't give employees anything to build on. They don't point out the specifics of ineffective behavior. They tend to make employees defensive, hurt, and perhaps angry. A better way is to change behavior by giving specific examples of where employees succeeded and where they failed.

- Evaluation is a once-a-year, cursory affair. It involves little planning and even less concern about the outcome.

- The performance appraisal process is linked to salary increases. These two should never be connected. Remember that the main purpose of performance appraisal is employee development. When it is understood by the employee that pay changes will be discussed at the end of the evaluation procedure, little of the meeting will be absorbed because he or she will be waiting for the "bottom line." If it is understood that pay will be discussed at another meeting, both of you can concentrate on developing skills.

- The manager starts an annual review at the end of the day or allows telephone interruptions. This signals to the employee that the review is not really important.

- The appraisal form consists of a series of boxes to be checked; it does not allow for individual expression. People don't like to be put into boxes of any kind. The best appraisal form is a blank piece of paper on which both the manager and the employee write how they see the employee's performance for the year.

- Everyone gets rated "Outstanding" or "Excellent." When this happens, either the manager is afraid to deal with realities or else the company has a tacit policy that no one is to be hurt.

If, as described in previous chapters, developing people is a continuous process, why do we need a formal appraisal program? First, in the absence of a required program, many managers just won't do anything. When these managers have to complete the form, they are confronted with the task of becoming people developers. Second, the process assures communication. Since the manager and employee both sign the form, at least some hope exists that they are hearing each other. Finally, adherence to a common process creates a company-wide cohesiveness and ensures that everyone is being treated in the same way.

Managing Performance Appraisal

Performance appraisal is more than just a chore to complete. It is an opportunity to develop your subordinates. It's a chance for you to help them achieve better results and increase their sense of fulfillment on the job. Some very specific methods work, others don't. Try some of these methods for a positive outcome:

- Never allow appraisal to become only an annual affair. Meet with and counsel your employees often. The actual appraisal should be nothing more than summarizing what you and they have been discussing all year. The test of a successful appraisal interview is this: there should be no surprises. You should simply be formalizing what both of you already know.

- Take all the time you need. Don't start an appraisal review shortly before quitting time. Signal that the person you are reviewing is important to you by cutting off telephones and other intrusions.

- Don't make the negative aspects of the appraisal punitive. When employees fail, be merciful and fire them. If you are going to retain such employees, you need to tell them you want them to change some of their behaviors. Tell them you value them and want to see them get ahead by improving their performance. People can feel good about negative feedback if they feel that their manager cares about them. (Very few parents have permanently alienated their children by administering well-deserved, carefully explained, correctly administered discipline accompanied by love.)

- If you have the courage, make appraisal a two-way street. Employees should feel free to openly acknowledge their perceptions of you, how the relationship could be improved, and how you can help them attain their goals. If you can do this openly, listen well, and have a meaningful interchange with the majority of your employees, you are on-track to becoming a very successful manager.

- The heart of good performance appraisal is goal setting. Study the information in Chapter 7. Then incorporate it into your appraisal in this way:

  1. Have employees set goals for a year in advance.
  2. In addition, set the goals you think they should accomplish.
  3. In the final review, agree on these goals.
  4. Use the goals as a standard to measure performance in next year's appraisal.

One way to hold down defensive reactions is to criticize the act but never the person. "You do some stupid things" is never okay. A better way is to say, "That incident on the Jones job didn't work out well because you didn't check out some of the details before you started. You may want to pay more attention to details on such jobs in the future."

- Ask yourself, "What do I expect this person to do?" Then communicate your expectations. If you do this thoughtfully and regularly, you set up the basis for an honest evaluation which includes no misunderstanding.

- Never assume that by giving out a lot of high ratings you will be seen by those about you as a good manager. The actual performance of your work group is the criterion by which you will be judged.

Making formal performance appraisals will be hardest the first year because you will not be working against goals. Set up a two-meeting process. In the first meeting, follow these steps:

Meeting I: The Appraisal

1. Before the meeting, ask your employee to write out a description of the job as he or she sees it. Have the employee include every task and responsibility and rank them according to their importance. Ask the employee to list any suggestions for self-improvement through training sessions, formal education, or other programs.

2. Make a file on this employee, writing up the job as you see it, and assess the employee's strengths against the tasks and responsibilities of the job.

3. Compare the employee's perception of the job with your own. Note any discrepancies between what the employee thinks the job is and what you think it is. Think through your ideas with the goal of developing the employee. When you have completed all of this preparation, you are ready for the meeting.

4. Set a time for your meeting and stick to it. Do everything you can to let your employee know that you consider this an important session. Let the employee know at the outset that the purpose of your getting together is to work on his or her development.

5. Compare notes — yours and the employee's. See where you agree and where you disagree. Try to reach a mutual understanding on priorities for the next year. In discussing areas where improvement is needed, don't be judgmental — just stick to specific examples.

6. Close the meeting on a positive note. Remember that the purpose of the meeting is to make this person a more effective employee, not to punish.

Since you have not been working against goals, the first formal appraisal is a meeting of minds. It should set you up for a good relationship in subsequent years, when you will use mutually agreed-on goals to make the appraisal process even more meaningful.

Meeting II: Setting Goals

1. Read through Chapter 7, "Goal Setting," very carefully. Make copies of any relevant parts and give them to your employee to read. Ask the employee to set goals for the coming year using the guidelines.

2. Write up the goals you feel this person should accomplish in the coming year. Weigh your suggestions carefully, keeping in mind both the company's needs and the employee's abilities.

3. Call your second meeting and compare notes. Between you, work out a set of goals that both of you can agree on. Discuss what the employee will need in order to reach those goals — help from you, cooperation from others, new resources, or training. Instruct the employee to rewrite the goals you both agreed on.

4. Hold the second part of the meeting when the rewrite is complete. Make sure everything is clear. Finish the meeting on an up-note.

What appears to be a time-consuming process may well be one of the most effective jobs you do as a manager. You now have two-way, open communication with your employees. They know how you see them, and you have developed a clear set of goals with each of them. They know where they are going and how to get there.

Completing the formal part is not the end of appraisal/development. During the course of the year you need to hold regular meetings to discuss employee progress. If necessary, rewrite goals to meet changing situations. The performance appraisal is now fulfilling its real function: communication and development.

The Second Year

In the second year, ask your employees to write out their job description and strengths assessment. Try adding a weaknesses assessment, too. If your employees can do this honestly, you know trust exists between you. Work hard toward this. Ask them to evaluate their performance against the goals. On your own, do the same. When you come together for your meeting, reach an agreement on how well goals were accomplished.

Discuss what kept things from being perfect and decide what changes are needed. Work out new development plans.

At your second meeting, set your goals for next year. By this time you should be better at defining goals and your employees should be getting better at accomplishing them.

Throughout the year, continue the pattern of consulting with employees on their goal achievement and on developing their abilities. If you and the other managers in your company do this faithfully, you will be getting the best out of your employees.

Note that the appraisal process has not mentioned pay increases. You should never discuss pay during a performance appraisal. The purpose of appraisal is to develop your employees' abilities through feedback, planning, and goal setting. Discussing pay puts you in the position of being counselor and judge at the same time, and this simply does not work.

Some weeks or months later, when the time comes to evaluate pay changes, you can discuss the company position on increases along with the individual's performance review. Obviously, evaluations are used in awarding merit increases and promotions, but in the interest of a harmonious relationship, you should both agree on pay issues just as you do on all other issues.

The final step in the evaluation process is completion of a form that goes into the employee's file. This form should always be signed by the employee, and the manager and the employee should each have a copy.

An important consideration is what type of form to use. Dozens of options are possible, but the best is still a blank sheet of paper on which the employee and manager set down their respective impressions of how well the employee has performed against goals, outlining areas that need improvement and how to accomplish these improvements. If you feel the need for a real form, collect some from other companies in your area and do a cut-and-paste.

Introducing a New Appraisal Program

Introducing a performance appraisal program for the first time often brings apprehension on the part of your employees. There is the potential for some difficult days, until everyone realizes that this is to be a development program rather than an attempt to punish someone.

One antidote is to keep communications open by having everyone informed. The following is an example of a statement to employees which covers most of the issues. You can adapt it to suit your style, or photocopy it directly from the book and pass it out to everyone.

Our Policy on Performance Reviews

We all want to know how we are doing on the job and how our career is progressing. One of the best ways to do this is through a regular, annual review.

Performance reviews are a two-way street — an opportunity to talk with management about how you view your job and how you would like to develop professionally. It's also an opportunity for management to give you feedback on your strengths and point out areas where your performance can be improved. The whole intent is to help you perform better and to give you opportunities to grow.

In the beginning a certain amount of discomfort is always present. Even the best managers or owners find it difficult to sit down with an employee and tell it like it is. It's a part of our culture. We learn to make things nice. That's not always healthy because it leaves people in the dark about where they stand. If you don't get feedback on how you are doing, you may keep on making the same mistakes. Similarly, telling you about performance that went well is important.

We said this is a two-way street. You're going to take part in all discussions. You will be able to express your feelings about your job in any way you wish. You are also going to be able to do a self-evaluation that becomes part of the appraisal process.

A good way to ensure that our program works is to make some mutual commitments.

1. Let's talk with each other, not at each other. Let's really listen to each other, too. Most people don't listen for fear they will hear something they don't want to hear. That's a bad habit we can all drop.

2. Let's stay focused on what this is about — doing a better job.

3. Let's remember we are all part of a team. We all need to pull together.

4. Let's be honest with each other, but not in a punishing way. Straight talk does not mean hurting or putting someone down.

We don't expect this will be a perfect process, but we do expect it to improve communication, let us look at how we are doing now, and help us see how we can do better in the future.

Questions about Performance Appraisal

Use these questions as a basis for a group discussion on performance appraisal.

1. What experiences have you had with performance appraisal? Which ones were most useful to you? Which were least useful?

2. What kinds of evaluations of others do we do most easily? Which are the most difficult?

3. Which areas covered in a performance appraisal are likely to be most sensitive?

4. What are some of the common prejudices that influence performance appraisal?

5. Is having subordinates evaluate the boss advantageous? How would you feel about this?

6. How do you decide which criteria to emphasize in a performance appraisal?

7. How can we get everyone to appreciate the value of performance appraisals?

Additional Information

Books

Pay People Right: Breakthrough Reward Strategies to Create Great Companies, Patricia Zingheim, Jossey-Bass, 2000. Compensation must be in alignment with a company's strategic goals.

Performance Appraisals for Business and Industry, George C. Morrisey, Addison-Wesley, 1983. Valuable book. Includes thoughts on legal considerations in performance appraisal.

What to do About Performance Appraisal, Marion S. Kellogg, Amacom, 1975. Good hands-on approach.

Resources

If you want to design a performance appraisal form for your company, call your local university faculty for copies they may have on file, or call the personnel offices of large companies in your area.

Note: Usually, performance appraisal falls into the area of personnel management, not management development. Look for other materials on performance appraisal under "personnel."

How to Interpret the Test for Chapter 8

If you wish to be a top-performing business owner or manager, you should be able to answer "Yes" to all ten questions.

Chapter 9

The Wellness Quiz

Do you lead a lifestyle that helps control stress? Your responses to these statements will offer a clearer picture. Information about responses to these questions is at the end of this chapter.

	Yes	No
1. The state of my health is an important component in how I live my life.	☐	☐
2. I don't smoke.	☐	☐
3. I meditate or do a deep-relaxation exercise at least fifteen minutes a day.	☐	☐
4. My personal relationships are satisfying.	☐	☐
5. I pay attention to the quality and quantity of the foods I eat.	☐	☐
6. I allow myself to feel and express a full range of emotions.	☐	☐
7. At times I allow myself to do nothing, without feeling guilty.	☐	☐
8. My life is challenging and exciting.	☐	☐
9. I have a high energy level.	☐	☐
10. Four or more times a week I do an aerobic exercise that lasts at least thirty minutes. I also do stretching and limbering exercises regularly.	☐	☐

Chapter 9

Managing Stress

The Impact of Stress

Stress! It impacts the lives of over 65 million Americans. More than five billion doses of tranquilizers and sleeping pills are consumed daily in the United States, in attempts to reduce its effects. Thirty million of us have been clinically diagnosed with acute anxiety disorders such as panic, phobias, and post-traumatic stress disorders, while 35 million of us suffer mild to moderate symptoms. A Harvard medical school study indicates that patients who cope poorly with stress are four times more likely to become physically ill than those with coping strategies that work for them.

Are these people who "just can't take it?" Many researchers don't think so. According to research done by Juliet Schor, professor of economics at Harvard, the average American is working 163 hours per year more than he or she worked in 1970. That's another full month! And if you are a management professional, the numbers are even higher.

What is Stress, Anyway?

According to Dr. Hans Selye, who first used the term in this context, stress is the sum of all the nonspecific effects of factors that can act upon the body. In other words, anything that affects the body in any way causes stress. The factors that cause stress are called stressors. Selye divided these stressors into external stressors and internal stressors, and while there is not really a clear line between them, suffice it to say that external stressors are those that originate in our environment and include everything from the people we are surrounded by to the food we eat. Internal stressors are those things that we bring to the present as a result of our past. Our beliefs, perceptions, and conditioning can all be examples of internal stressors. Our stress reactions can be seen as the result of the interplay between these two kinds of stressors.

The same stressors affect different individuals in different ways. According to Dr. Murray Mittleman of Boston's Beth Israel Medical Center, one of the strongest stressors that managers face is working under a high-pressure deadline. But while one manager may respond to such a stressor by having heart problems, another may react to the same stressor by getting migraines or ulcers, while a third may have lower back pain.

Here is where the "nonspecific" part of Selye's definition of stress comes in. Any stressor has the effect of stimulating the body's sympathetic nervous system. In turn, the sympathetics put all of the body's major organs on alert, i.e., under stress. Whatever organ is the weakest in the system becomes the most stressed. Unless this stress can be discharged in some way, the steady dose of stress-inducing hormones can cause illness, and eventually premature death. Selye called this cycle the General Adaptation Syndrome (GAS).

Fight or Flight

During the early years of the century, the great Harvard physiologist Walter B. Cannon was able to experimentally prove what everyone had long suspected: man, like the rest of the mammals, has a built-in response to perceived stressors. Cannon called it the "fight or flight response." In the presence of danger — or what is perceived as danger — the body immediately goes into survival mode. While in this mode, the heart rate and blood pressure increase, capillaries dilate, forcing blood away from the extremities, the stomach contracts, causing vomiting in extreme cases, and respiration increases, forcing more oxygen into the bloodstream for the efforts to come. These reactions prepare the body to either run or fight.

Unless restrained in some way, animals will discharge their stressor-induced hormone cocktail by running or fighting. But what happens when they are restrained or in some other way prevented from acting in the manner that their physiology requires? In his experiments with rats, Selye discovered that when placed in situations of unrelieved stress, rats would develop ulcers, heart disease, arthritis, and cancer, just to name the easily-observable diseases. This is what can happen if the general adaptation syndrome is allowed to run its course.

Cannon, Selye, and the stress researchers that followed them have found that human beings react to an undischarged stress buildup in the same way that other animals do: we develop symptoms of chronic stress. If these are left unchecked, we can develop some of the same stress-related diseases that Selye observed in his experimental animals.

So, if the lives we have created for ourselves make it difficult or impossible to follow our bodies' dictates for running or fighting, perhaps one answer to a less stressful life is to learn to avoid as much stress as we can. Believe it or not, there actually are some effective ways to do this at work and in our personal lives as well.

Coping Strategies

Ben Franklin said, "Time is the stuff life is made of." As true as that is, few of us actually organize our time in ways that keep us in control of it, rather than the other way around. One reason for this is the way we perceive events around us. Often, we have learned to see ourselves in the center of a fire ring, battling flames in all directions, our extinguisher almost depleted. While we cannot control all the events in our lives, many of today's fires are the result of previous decisions we made about allocating our time.

Learn to prioritize your time. For one week, keep a log of how you spend your time at work. Do it in ten-minute increments. Don't attempt to change anything yet — just log how you are currently spending your time. After a week, analyze your log. You will be shocked at the amount of time you spend on items that are either not important or could be done by others. Avoid stress by giving yourself time to do those things that are important first. Then allocate time to make more informed decisions about the urgent matters. By the way, just staring out the window may need to be on your important list.

There is another value to making a time log. It can give you an idea of things you do every day that you may be quite unconscious of doing. Some of these may be adding to your stress. For example, is your time going to and from work a time of calmness and relaxation, or do you use these minutes to pump up your anxiety? Many people feel they should use their time in traffic to make calls to clients or the office. Others listen to a news station the whole time. Instead, try listening to music or to a book on tape or CD. Use the time between home and work and work and home as a time to relax. But what about traffic? you may ask. Your whole perspective on your day can shift positively if you leave fifteen minutes earlier than scheduled.

Designate a specific time each day to answer e-mail and return telephone calls. If you don't use a planner already, consider getting one and learning to use it. Hiram Smith, founder of the Franklin Institute, suggests blocking out a period of time every day where your secretary or assistant can make appointments for you. That way, you can control the rest of your time without being concerned about appointments you may have overlooked.

Directly related to managing your time is learning to delegate tasks to others. Believing that you are the only one who can do it right puts unrelenting pressure on everyone and is a major cause of stress-induced illness. Therefore, one of the most effective ways for executives to avoid stress is to delegate. Many managers believe that they delegate a lot. After all, don't they hand off work to their subordinates? Yes, but for the most part, giving subordinates work to do is a very different process than delegation. Delegation requires that a manager give the responsibility for completing the whole task, or at least a significant portion, to somebody else. While most, if not all of your employees can complete tasks under supervision, a far smaller number may be ready for the responsibility of delegation. For more on this see Chapter 6.

Another long-term strategy to avoid executive stress is to let many of the decisions regarding how work should be done be made by those close to the work. An effective way to do this is by building work teams that meet to discuss how work flow and processes can be implemented and improved. As with delegation, employees need training to work well together in groups. After studying scores of teams and work groups, we have concluded that successful groups take responsibility for the work they do and focus on the process — the way they go about relating to one another as decisions are made — as much as they focus on the task to be done. Just keep in mind that effective teams let employees help you avoid stress by taking the responsibility to help themselves. For suggestions about team building see Chapter 3.

From the perspective of your life as a whole, the most effective way of avoiding stress is to become more self-aware. The more you are able to monitor your internal reactions to your environment, the easier it will be for you to identify the stressors in your life and take steps to reduce or eliminate them completely. Many have found that some form of meditation is a way to accomplish this. Take some of the time you found when you did your time log and use it for something really important.

There are many methods of meditation, but a simple, easy one to learn, adapted by Herbert Benson at Harvard University, is to simply close your eyes, relax, and repeat a word or phrase that you find relaxing. It can be something scriptural like "The Lord is my shepherd," or a word like "calming." Benson found that this simple exercise can have a measurable impact on stress-related symptoms such as heart rate and blood pressure. The effects of meditating twice a day for ten minutes are long-lasting, and will help you increase your awareness of your inner reactions to the stressors around you, an important first step in learning to avoid them.

Another method is deep relaxation. Many Americans prefer this because it is more of a "doing" process, rather than the simply "being" process of meditation. You will find a complete guide to deep relaxation at the end of this chapter.

Scientists have always been aware of the effect that the mind can have on the body, but only lately has there been enough empirical evidence to thoroughly support it. The unconscious mind has no voice; it speaks to each of us through the language of the body. It is up to us to learn to understand this language and follow its promptings.

The Wellness Model

Until recently, experts advised that you either remove the stressors from your environment or remove yourself from the stressors. New evidence says stress is not the problem; it is our response to it that largely determines health or sickness. Studies of executives under stress showed that those who stayed well were optimistic about life and had a sense that they had control over things and events. They were all deeply involved in their work and families and had a commitment that gave them meaning, direction, and excitement. Essentially, they had adopted a positive attitude or belief. Even though we cannot always control objective reality, we can learn how to react to it. People at peace with themselves and their immediate surroundings usually remain in good health!

The wellness model implies a continuum scale rather than an either/or, sick-or-well choice. It includes both psychological wellness and physical wellness, in other words, the well-being of the whole person. Further, it assumes your health depends almost entirely on what you do with your body and your mind.

If you stuff your body with junk food, cigarette smoke, drugs, and other toxic substances, this is a choice you make. Similarly, how you handle your emotions, your relationships, and your work affects your health and can be changed by choice. By taking the wellness path, you learn to act and live in ways that can bring you feelings of exuberance, vitality, joy, and fulfillment.

In the treatment model, the opposite of the wellness model, the standard is the absence of disease. In this model, the physician is responsible for your health. In the wellness model, you are responsible.

Our view, and that of many of our national leaders, is that the wellness model is one of the most important concepts of our time. Certainly, the treatment model has failed us. This is evident in our out-of-hand medical costs, and our excessively high early-death rate. The wellness model offers us a way to become proactive in our lives, to gain control over our health, to reduce the impact of stress, and to enjoy a continual sense of well-being.

Eat Well, Breathe Well, and Move Well

The wellness model shows us that we need to focus as much on the quality of energy we put into our system as we do on reducing the number of things that stress us. There are three methods by which we input life energy into our bodies — eating, breathing, and moving. The more we understand the nature of each of these, the more energy we will have available for living and the less stress we will experience. Through scientific research, we are learning that each cell in the body has a life of its own as well as being part of the network that supports us. The more we can nourish our cells by proper eating, breathing, and moving, the more awake and alive each cell can be, and the more effective the cell network will become in withstanding the impact of stressors.

Eating

A great deal of our energy is spent digesting the foods we eat. Hard-to-digest foods such as animal protein take greater amounts of energy than foods like vegetables and fruits. That does not mean that we will be healthier if we do not eat meat. Actually, that seems to depend on the individual; some bodies seem to need more meat than others. Recent studies, though, seem to indicate that vegetables, salads, and fruit cut down the risk of serious disease even in meat-eaters. Experiment with cutting back your meat intake and see how you feel.

While we are not advocating a meatless diet, there are some interesting stress-related data indicating that it may have some value. People who consume animal products are forty percent more susceptible to cancer and at increased risk for many other illnesses, including stroke, obesity, appendicitis, osteoporosis, arthritis, diabetes, and food poisoning.

In addition, meat contains accumulations of pesticides and other chemicals that are up to fourteen times more concentrated than those in plant foods. As pointed out in the Journal of Cardiology, people on a vegetarian diet can become "heart attack proof" over time by being able to lower their cholesterol to below 150, a level at which few heart attacks have been recorded.

Another interesting fact about diet and its relation to stress is that under stressful conditions, many people crave foods filled with sugar and fat—the very foods that research has shown are linked to placing your system under more stress. Stress also causes increased consumption of tobacco and alcohol in some people. So, the more stress you experience, the more likely it is that you will ingest substances that cause more stress. Consider that it may be easier to break this cycle by controlling the substances you ingest than by focusing only on the stressors in your environment.

Breathing

Most of us are unaware of the way we breathe. We know that oxygen in the air we breathe keeps us alive, but that's about as far as it goes. Actually, the way in which we breathe determines how deeply we react to stressors. In stressful circumstances we tend to breathe in a shallow

manner, limiting the amount of oxygen available to brain cells and causing oxygen starvation. As a result, we cannot think clearly. Under extreme
stress, the chest constricts and the diaphragm freezes up, causing hyper-
ventilation and panic. In other words, our body reacts to the changes in
oxygen level as much as to the stressor itself.

The act of breathing is the only bodily function that is both voluntary and
involuntary. The intake of air goes on without our conscious control most
of the time, but it can be taken over by our consciousness smoothly and
without effort. As a result, we can learn to control the amount of oxygen
that gets to our cells under conditions of stress. So if that is the case, why
don't we do that and thus limit the amount of impact stress has on our
minds and bodies?

There are two related reasons why we usually don't. The first is habit.
Observe any animal (including yourself) when a possible stressor
appears in the environment. The animal stops, scans, and then moves
accordingly, either assuming the fight or flight mode or ignoring the
sound or smell. For those few moments, the animal holds its breath in
order to shut down the internal "noise" so that the external will take the
foreground. If there is no threat, normal breathing begins again. But if it
is not clear whether the sound or smell is threatening or not, breathing
becomes shallow, allowing just enough air to keep the body functioning,
but not enough internal noise to be distracting. This continues until it is
determined whether there is a need for action or not. In an environment
where there are many potential threats or stressors, the shallow breathing
may continue and become a habit.

The second reason relates to what we said above about oxygen starvation. When the brain cells are not sufficiently nourished by oxygen, we
tend to think less clearly. In other words, it may not occur to us to take
conscious control of the breath cycle and bring more oxygen into the system. We can learn to be more proactive in this regard through practice,
associating stressful situations with the need to increase our breathing.

Moving

There are two ways that movement and stress are connected. The first we
have talked about before — the way that movement is triggered by the
fight or flight response, and how stress accumulates in the body when circumstances preclude either running or fighting. The second connection

relates to what we have discussed above about breathing. Any movement puts a certain amount of stress on the body. That demand triggers the body's need for more oxygen. As a result, the diaphragm and lungs cooperate by sucking in more air. The higher the demand put on the system by running or lifting, for example, the more oxygen is picked up from the lungs and transferred to the cells by the bloodstream. The more we move, the more we oxygenate and enliven our cells. The more alive our cells are, the less susceptible we are to the ravages of stressful living. It's that simple. It isn't necessary to engage in strenuous exercise for benefits to accrue. Walking, stretching, skipping rope, and swimming all can help. Exercise coupled with better eating and breathing habits will greatly improve your quality of life.

Deep Relaxation

One major tool to reduce stress and optimize wellness is the ability to go into a state of deep relaxation (DR). Used regularly each day for a period of approximately fifteen minutes, it has the potential to offset many hours of stressful work. In the DR state, you feel physically relaxed and detached from the world. You experience a feeling of letting go, of abandoning your worries and cares. You can use the DR state to achieve a sense of emptiness and floating, or it can be used for mind control in a program of wellness and growth. Many of the wellness-based healing techniques make use of life-enhancing benefits that start from a state of deep relaxation.

Deep relaxation is a profoundly restful state. It can give you new energy, a sense of peacefulness, and can act as a buffer against the intrusions of the day. Many people are surprised to discover they carry chronic tenseness in their bodies and enjoy learning a positive way to let go. You can use any of several relaxation techniques. An easy one to learn is Progressive Relaxation. Using a systematic sequence, you can learn to relax each of the muscle groups in your body. After following this method for a few weeks, you will find you can go into DR just by sitting or lying comfortably, closing your eyes, then taking several deep breaths and counting down from ten to zero. You will find complete instructions for going into the DR state later in this chapter.

We have taught the DR technique to hundreds of students, executives, and managers with excellent results. Those who practice DR regularly report an extraordinary ability to cope with the stressors in their environment, a new inner peace, and a feeling of pure pleasure about themselves. Deep relaxation is recommended to you as one of the major steps on your path to wellness.

Once you have learned to slip easily into a state of DR, you can begin visualization exercises to improve general wellness or to accomplish healing. Earlier you learned about the mind-body connection. With this knowledge, you can understand how to enhance your immune system by programming your mind. This can be done simply and effectively through the visualization process. In the DR state, you can evoke specific imagery to deal with any health problem.

Much research has been done on visualization, and it promises many possibilities in autogenic healing.

Enhance Your Well-Being

The wellness model is a whole-person approach. The medical treatment model regards the mind and emotions as separate from the body, and most physicians treat the part of the person they can get their hands on. From the wellness viewpoint, a person is one entity — mind-body-spirit. To be fully healthy, you need to understand that the emotional (psychological) is inseparable from the physical. Paying attention to the affective is equally as important as eating right, exercising, and practicing DR. Consider these things when working on your psychological well-being:

- Total wellness is a question of balance. Many people become lopsided workaholics whose only rewards come from the job. Well people have time for play, relationships, time alone, service, and other activities.

- Check your commitments. Accept and follow through on those that have meaning for you. Drop the rest.

- Associate with people who add to your life. Rethink your friendships. Drop the ones that are unrewarding. The most valuable relationships are those that allow you to be who you truly are.

- Take some time to be alone.

- Make sure you are learning something new, having new experiences, going beyond your everyday routine. Some of the most exciting people we know are going back to school at age forty, fifty, or older.

- Build a support team. Share your inner feelings with your family or have a group of friends who affirm you. In the wellness process, nothing beats real love relationships.

- Think positive. Some of the most important research of our time shows that our experience is shaped by our perceptions. That is, our world tends to be what we expect it to be. Foot-draggers and naysayers dig themselves into holes. Check this out for yourself. Just replace all the negative images and thoughts in your mind with positive thoughts and affirmations. Watch how things change for you.

- Nurture the child in you. Let go and be playful now and then. Laugh at your own mistakes. If you need any help with this, just follow around and emulate a child for a day. Being too serious has severe limitations.

- Welcome change. Change is all around us. Resisting change is like trying to swim upstream. It's much more natural to go with the flow.

- Find new ways to express your creativity. Get unstuck. Don't keep doing things the same way.

- Expand your awareness. Stop running on automatic and tune in to your inner feelings. A good way to do this is to breathe consciously from time to time. Focusing on your breathing helps you to go inside and contact your senses.

- Look for some deeper meaning in your life. Explore your spiritual side and its importance for you.

- Love yourself. Appreciate yourself for who you are. Acknowledge your accomplishments. Enjoy the beauty inside you.

The best manager is the best person. The well person manages well.

A Guide to Low-Stress Managing

While this book is about successful management of people, it is also about being a low-stress manager of people. If you manage in the style this book advocates, you will be less stressed and your employees will be less stressed. This means healthier people, higher productivity, and more profits. Now that you have a good idea how to handle your own stress and create your own wellness program, consider how to be a manager in a low-stress environment.

A good way to become a low-stress manager is to examine the problems, attitudes, and fears that people bring with them to the workplace. Understanding these, you can include in your management style ways to help your people cope.

- All people need to feel in control of their lives to be healthy. Feeling that you can do nothing, that no matter what happens you have no power, is the basis for most depression. Many people feel this way about their lives, and when these feelings are exacerbated at work the chances of a physical breakdown increase. As a manager, you can empower others by delegating as much responsibility as you can. With delegation goes autonomy and a degree of freedom. Similarly, letting employees participate in management decisions that affect their area of work gives them real power and real control.

- Many people bring to the job a gunnysack full of repressed anger. Some people's gunnysacks are stuffed so full that their every utterance is hostile. Causes can be rooted in early childhood and perpetuated in a society where venting anger is not acceptable. You can't have everyone running around yelling, but you can avoid adding to what is already a considerable burden for many of your employees. The best escape valve is open communication and a real open-door policy, where people are encouraged to express their feelings without fear of reprisal. The opportunity to tell it like it is in a supportive environment is healthy for everyone.

- Many people, down deep, don't feel very good about themselves. The causes run the gamut from parental abuse to the finger-pointing of teachers. As a manager, you can keep this situation from getting worse by acknowledging good work. Look for reasons to praise someone honestly and do it with a smile and a thank you. This bit of attention to a real human need is one of the cheapest, easiest, and most powerful management tools.

- A lot of people feel disconnected and look to the job to satisfy their need to belong. You've heard about being lonely in a crowd. Workplaces can be the most alienating places of all. In the midst of a large or small company, too many people feel left out and ignored. One good tool for correcting this problem is the collaborative group (see Chapter 3). Number one on the "feel good" list is the opportunity to collaborate with others on a goal-oriented task. This produces a valuable sense of belonging.

- Practically everyone fears change. Anxiety about the unknown is a top stress-producer. That's why people hang on to the old, tested ways so rigidly. When you plan changes, include those concerned in any planning. If they are involved in the process, they will have less to fear. (See Chapter 12.)

- One of the prime causes of stress reactivity is a promotion. That's okay if the stress disappears after the person becomes familiar with the new job, but often it doesn't. Instead it becomes chronic, and the person may try to escape through alcohol or drugs. Promotion is seen in our society as an honor, but to some people, it's a sentence. Moral: Never promote someone without his or her concurrence. Make sure to leave a graceful way out and don't penalize the employee if the promotion is refused. If the employee accepts the promotion, monitor the situation from time to time to see that all is going well.

- Rivalry creates apprehension in most people, terror in some. In our good American way, we foster competition so we can see the cream rise. Unfortunately, that leaves the majority to sink. Rivalry becomes something quite different when it's us (our company) against them (our competition). Then, we draw on the strength of the group, as opposed to a one-on-one struggle. The idea here is to keep internal competition to a minimum, using the strength of the team to tackle the external competition.

- "What am I supposed to do around here?" Role ambiguity is highly correlated with the kind of prolonged, free-floating anxiety that produces stress-related illness. In many companies, clear job descriptions are unavailable. People in these companies don't know where their job begins and ends or, more important, what is expected of them. The answer is in clear job descriptions, jointly created by you and the employee, and in goal setting, so that all employees know where they are going and what is expected.

- "No one ever tells me where I stand." Lack of feedback causes stress. Employees need to know how they are doing. This issue is discussed thoroughly in Chapter 8.

Other stressors arise, too: being in a dead-end job with no hope of getting anywhere; feeling that management doesn't care about you; and a host of others. By now you understand that stress management is interrelated with every other management activity and managing your own stress comes before managing others. A company's health is irrevocably intertwined with the health of the people who make it go.

A Deep Relaxation Guide

As a preliminary to deep relaxation, decide on the length of time you wish to spend. Fifteen minutes is average — you can go to twenty or more if you wish. Look at your watch and note what time it will be when you plan to complete your exercise. Tell yourself that you will awaken refreshed at the indicated time. If you do this at the beginning of every relaxation period, you will soon find that you have a built-in alarm clock that will awaken you automatically when the time is up. With this assurance, you can do your exercise any time or place, knowing you will be up and going for your next appointment. Stick with it. Setting your internal alarm requires a few weeks of repetition.

You can make up your own relaxation technique or you can use the one that follows. After you have used instructions for a few weeks you will be able to sink easily into deep relaxation simply by closing your eyes, breathing deeply, and counting backwards slowly from ten to zero.

Whenever you begin DR find a quiet place where you know you won't be interrupted. You may lie down, but sitting up in a chair works equally well. Make sure that your legs are uncrossed and your hands are in a comfortable position. Take your glasses off. If you lie down, lie flat with your head supported. If you sit, use the full back of the chair as support. Don't slouch.

Tape-record the following instructions. You can have someone make the tape for you, or you can tape it yourself. You may wish to have some gentle music playing in the background. Record the instructions slowly. The ellipses (…) indicate places to pause.

> *Just allow your eyes to close …*
>
> *Begin by taking relaxation breaths … breathe in deeply through your nose and out through your mouth …*
>
> *With each outgoing breath, imagine that all the tensions and cares of the day flow out of your body … repeat the relaxation breath several times … breathe in deeply through your nose and out through your mouth …*
>
> *Now, focus your attention on your feet and just let them relax …*
> *Just let go from your toes to your heels …*

Take the deep relaxation up into your legs, allowing all tension to flow down through your feet and out through your toes ...

Take the relaxation into your thighs, just letting go ...

This is a time for just being ... nowhere to go, nothing to do ...

Now, take the relaxation into your midsection, being aware of the rising and falling of your abdomen as you breathe the relaxation into your body ... just letting go ...

As the relaxation flows into your chest, just be aware of your breathing and let it relax you ...

Take the relaxation into the back of your neck and the back of your shoulders ... this is a place where you often store tension, so you might wish to imagine that any tension you are holding melts into liquid and just let it drain down into your arms and out your fingers ... just let it go ...

Now, take the relaxation and let it go down your back in little ripples, allowing each vertebra to relax ...

Let the relaxation move to your shoulders and run down through your arms and fingers ...

Now the relaxation moves up the back of your head ... across the top ... down your forehead and across your eyes ... down through your cheekbones and into your mouth ...

Check your throat, too, and let any tension go ... become aware now of the wonderful feeling as your body is becoming fully relaxed, yet your mind is very alert ...

To go deeper into relaxation, imagine you are standing at the top of a stairway, or a down escalator, or an elevator if you wish ... and as you go down, each count will take you deeper and deeper into relaxation ... 10 ... 9 ... 8 ... 7 ... 6 ... 5 ... 4 ... 3 ... 2 ... 1 ... 0.

Find yourself, magically, in your favorite place of relaxation ... in the mountains, by the seashore, in the desert, wherever you like ... or make one up ...a very special place for you alone ... let it be a place that is outdoors ... beautiful, peaceful, serene, and secure ... a magical special place ...

Sense it as fully as you can ... Can you see a bright yellow sun blazing in the sky? ... Can you feel its golden warmth on your body? ... how good it feels ... Is the sky a bright, dazzling blue, with white puffy clouds floating by? ... Sense the beauty all around you ... feel the gentle breeze ... breathe in the clean, fresh air ... feel how it relaxes you ... how good this place feels ... just enjoy it ...

Look around and see if you can find a favorite spot ... where you can just be one with the peacefulness of your special place ...

Go there and stretch out ... enjoy it ... in this beautiful place of your own you can be fully at peace ...

As you rest and relax you can feel all the magic of this place as it does special things for you ... restoring, nourishing, energizing, healing ... Take a few moments to enjoy your special place ... (long pause) ...

As you experience how wonderful it is to be here, tell yourself that you can return any time you wish, simply by taking a few minutes to relax yourself, and then letting your imagination carry you here ...

Each time you come to visit you will find it more serene, more beautiful, more peaceful ... it's available to you any time you wish ...

Before leaving, tell yourself that when you end this experience you will feel not only rested, relaxed, and comfortable, but also full of such a powerful sense of well being that you will feel easily able to take on any challenge of the day ... (long pause) ...

To end this experience just count from one to five, and on the count of five come fully awake, feeling rested, refreshed, well ... 1 ... 2 ... 3 ... 4 ... 5.

Do any variation of this exercise that suits you, always finding your way to your private relaxation place. If you practice DR every day, in a short time you will have a peacefulness that you can carry with you or call up anytime you want. Whenever you are in a tense situation, take a few deep breaths, let them out very slowly, and relaxation will flow over you. You are now the owner of a powerful wellness tool. Use it well.

Assessing Risk Factors

Complete this form and refer to it from time to time as a way to guide your personal health program.

My Personal Risk Factors

What factors in your current health and self-care patterns are presently causing difficulty in your life or are likely to cause problems in the future? What patterns, if continued, will diminish the quality of your life one year from now? Ten years from now?

Physical

_____

_____

Mental

_____

_____

Emotional

_____

_____

Social

_____

_____

Spiritual

_____

_____

Lifestyle

_____

_____

Additional Information

Books on Stress

Stress Management for Busy People, Carol Turkington and David Barlow, McGraw-Hill, 1998. Stress management and stress reduction techniques.

Stress Without Distress, Hans Selye, Signet, 1975. By the seminal researcher in the field. Provides background for understanding the physiology of stress.

Books about the Mind-Body Connection

Everyday Serenity: Meditations for People Who Do Too Much, David Kuntz, Conan Press, 1999. Offers a welcome respite for anyone perpetually in overdrive.

Healing and the Mind, Bill Moyers, Doubleday, 1993. From Moyer's television series, a comprehensive study of the mind-body connection.

Ageless Body, Timeless Mind, Deepak Chopra, M.D., Harmony Books, 1993. Mind-body medicine combined with anti-aging research.

Head First: The Biology of Hope, Norman Cousins, Dutton, 1989. Scientific evidence that the mind can help mobilize the body's healing resources.

Minding the Body, Mending the Mind, Joan Borysenko, Bantam, 1988. How to take control of your own physical and mental well-being.

Books about Visualization

Health Journeys for People Experiencing Stress, Belleruth Naparstek, Time Warner Audio Books, 2000. Audio cassette with four exercises to reduce anxiety and maintain balance and calm.

Healing Visualizations, Gerald Epstein, Bantam, 1989. A comprehensive guide to image therapy for everything from the common cold to cancer.

Imagery in Healing, Jeanne Achterberg, New Science Library, 1985. How the systematic use of mental imagery can have a positive influence on disease states.

Directing the Movies of Your Mind, Adelaide Bry, Harper and Row, 1978. Contains precisely the images to create for wellness.

Books on Wellness

Office Yoga: Simple Stretches for Busy People, Darrin Zeer, Chronicle Books, 2000. A day planner for relaxation.

Wellness Workbook, 2nd ed., John W. Travis and Regina Sara Ryan, Ten Speed Press, 1989. Packed with information, tests, and charts. Interesting and challenging. The "wellness index" can give you a complete picture of how you rate on wellness.

Love, Medicine & Miracles, Bernie S. Siegel, Harper and Row, 1986. A surgeon writes about the healing power of love.

How to Interpret the Test for Chapter 9

Most Americans answer "Yes" to fewer than half these questions, yet adequate stress control calls for "Yes" on all ten.

You might wonder why we've included a chapter on Managing Stress in a book about managing people. Today's business environment is so demanding and so chaotic that it creates immense pressure, even for the most hardy. The result is a high incidence of illness in the workplace with concomitant human suffering and a major loss of productivity. Business leaders must learn how to cope with the stressors in their own lives and understand how their leadership style may contribute to excessive stress on their staff.

Chapter 10

Try Your Knowledge of Organizations on This

The study of organizational culture has been primarily confined to professionals in the field of organization development. Its introduction at the management level is very recent. Take the test as a way of beginning to build your knowledge of the subject, but don't be concerned if you fail to score high in this relatively new area. To assess your score, see the last page of this chapter.

	Yes	No
1. The culture of an organization can be summed up as "the way we do things around here."	☐	☐
2. Learning to manage the organization's culture is as important as managing the finances, marketing, and other business aspects.	☐	☐
3. Older organizations with well-defined cultures may be difficult to change.	☐	☐
4. Whether something as abstract as culture can be readily identified is not clear.	☐	☐
5. Often, an organization has many subcultures.	☐	☐
6. The values and beliefs of the original founders of the organization are very important in defining the culture that evolves.	☐	☐
7. An important consideration for the leaders in a merger or acquisition is the meshing of the two cultures.	☐	☐
8. Even well-conceived strategic plans cannot be implemented if they run against powerful cultural assumptions.	☐	☐
9. The understanding of organizational culture leads to better management of cultural diversity.	☐	☐
10. Knowledge of an organization's culture is helpful in selecting career employment.	☐	☐

Chapter 10

Understanding Culture

Valuing Culture

Culture is the shared behavior, norms, values, and assumptions that knit an organization together. It's the rules of the game, the unseen and often unspoken meaning that unifies everyone. It is often exemplified in the statement, "This is the way we do things around here." Any definable group with a shared history can have a culture, so within an organization there can be many subcultures. If the organization as a whole has had shared experiences, there will also be a total organizational culture.

That each organization, except those with only a brief history, has a workplace culture becomes very clear when you think about the feeling of being an outsider when first joining a company. It's like being in a foreign land. You have to learn how the system works, what's valued, how achievement is recognized. Gradually you gain a sense of the feel, the ambiance, the way of working, but transferring this understanding to words is difficult.

Such is the abstract nature of organizational culture. It is a complex phenomenon, not easy to measure or simple to define. Yet executives or managers who have an understanding of the culture in which they operate have a framework for making decisions that can be successfully carried out. This insight also allows them to ease growth or institute change in the human side of the organization.

A company's culture evolves through five patterns: (1) the unique history of a company (what products or services it offers, what successes it has achieved, what it has learned about its special competencies); (2) the values and deeply held beliefs of top management; (3) the beliefs of its employees; (4) the design of the management systems (the way communications flow, methods of compensation, the degree to which people participate in decisions); (5) critical success factors in the industry (those competencies an organization must have to be able to survive).

The Power of Culture

The history of a company often determines how powerful a culture becomes. If the founders have a clear, strong vision of where the company is headed and if the vision is clearly articulated so that it becomes the modus operandi throughout the organization, then unity of purpose will drive strategic decisions.

When no firm hand grips the steering wheel, or when managers or self-managed teams do not have a guiding philosophy, a variety of subcultures may form. One may then argue in favor of a strong culture. Yet this has a down-side: When conditions dictate substantial change in corporate direction, the entrenched culture may inhibit the necessary moves. Some even maintain that strong cultures in large organizations are immutable. Studies of large organizational development projects show that it is, indeed, difficult to dramatically change a culture.

AT&T, as it went through its first breakup and forced change in a strategic direction, found it needed many years to alter its century-old culture to one that was marketing oriented. The variety of values, behaviors, and assumptions that had to change for AT&T to maintain its market position was staggering. Similarly, McDonnell Douglas, in the 1980s, dictated that its culture be altered to conform more with the team model. Changing the hearts and minds of its managers was a formidable task. Then a second cultural shift was necessary when it merged with Boeing.

Many organizations are making substantial changes in the way they do business to remain competitive in the fast-moving global environment. They are finding that the entrenched way of doing things — the corporate culture — often stands in the way. The lesson is that understanding and managing organizational culture is as important as managing finances, the product, the physical plant, and marketing. Not only does culture limit strategic options, but you cannot carry out strategies that run against powerful assumptions.

The Ideal Culture

This book, in various ways, has been describing two cultural models. The Traditional Management model is characterized by a rigidly defined hierarchy, standardized control, power concentration at the top, internal competition, downward communication, individual versus team effort, carrot-and-stick motivation, low risk, and resistance to change.

The New Management model honors participative decision-making, collaboration, teamwork, intrinsic motivators, upward and lateral as well as downward communication, autonomy, encouragement of risk, innovation, mutual trust, and constant change. The New Management, employing shared values and beliefs, is optimally effective to meet the challenge of the global business environment and to satisfy the demands of people in the internal environment.

The Leader's Role in Early Culture Formation

Consider the case of John, who is the guiding light in the formation of a new hi-tech company: The venture capitalists examine him and his plan thoroughly and find his concept plausible, his engineering talent excellent, his desire to succeed admirable. The venture is funded and gets underway.

Our young leader is methodical and likes to take charge. He sets up a hierarchy where orders and information pass up and down the chain of command. He gathers information, then makes decisions himself. Most of them turn out well and he is soon the new darling of the media; word of his successes spreads across the nation. Wall Street recognizes his ability and the stock soars.

Ten years pass. Massive changes have occurred in our entrepreneur's industry. His original technology has been refined many times, but is now obsolete. The multi-million dollar corporation needs a radically new strategic direction. The Board of Directors removes John in favor of a new CEO with a solid track record of turning around ailing companies. The new CEO begins to work on products that require new manufacturing and marketing methods. But nothing works and things go from bad to worse. Does all of this seem familiar?

In a tight hierarchical organization, new initiatives require multiple approvals. The structure set up by the founder reinforces a culture of low risk-taking, since the process of obtaining all the necessary approvals can expose an individual to a series of potential challenges from superiors. The stories that go around the organization are the heroic deeds of the founder and the glory days which, additionally, fosters a "this is the way we always do it around here" aspect within the culture. This adds up to a culture too difficult to change in the available time, and another highly-touted American company bites the dust just ten years after it began.

Now consider the same case with Beth, an entrepreneur schooled in organizational culture. Looking toward the future, she sets up a flat organization with many self-managed small teams, a compensation system that rewards results over the long haul, and a management style that fosters innovation at all levels. The result is an organization able to move quickly and effectively with changing times.

When one examines the history of successful and unsuccessful organizations, the imprint of the founders is always an important factor.

The Leader's Role in Cultural Clarity

To perform effectively, leaders, at any level, must understand the concept of organizational culture and be able to diagnose correctly the culture in which they work. This is a real challenge, because observing a culture while still immersed in it is extremely difficult. Following are some guiding thoughts for the exploration of culture. Later in this chapter you will find specifics to help analyze your company.

- Culture is a very powerful shared reality. Each member becomes part of the culture and views the world from that perspective. The managers in a given culture are usually unable to see alternatives because of the control that the culture exerts on their perceptions and behavior. Staying aware of this problem allows them to be dispassionate observers while still operating within the culture.

- Watch that you don't oversimplify. Many culture-watchers rely on the obvious, such as artifacts and observable behavior. These are helpful, but the true test of a culture is in the basic assumptions or beliefs held by the leaders of the organization. These are mostly unobservable and bringing them to light takes some real detective work.

- Two kinds of beliefs are prevalent: "driving beliefs" and "daily beliefs." Driving beliefs are the principles top management applies. They are the bedrock on which the company is built. In contrast to driving beliefs, daily beliefs are day-to-day operational choices that influence individual behavior on the job. They are "how the game is played," the way tasks are performed. Driving beliefs are principles for formulating strategy; daily beliefs are the key to implementing strategy. In analyzing culture, do not confuse them.

- If a company does not have enough stability or common history, it may not have a defined, overarching culture. Frequent turnover of members also muddies a culture. This lack of a clear culture is common in organizations that are reactive, those that muddle along with no sense of direction or purpose, or in organizations without clearly articulated objectives.

- When analyzing why things are not going well, most managers dig into financial issues, equipment, marketing, the impact of the business environment — those items most commonly watched. The aware manager will also examine the organizational culture and its fit to current and long-range goals.

- When seeking new employment, aware managers choose companies where the driving beliefs match their own.

- Once the complexities of organizational culture are understood, the manager has a solid foundation for dealing with multicultural workforces, domestically or globally. (See Chapter 11 for more on this.)

- Executives are in a better position to manage the culture and adapt to rapid change in the environment when they have established an awareness of culture in their teams.

- Every manager at every level has a part to play in culture formation and management. Managerial vision can be an inspiration and catalyst, whether for a 3-person team in an accounting office or a for a 3,000-person manufacturing division. Managers can foster teamwork within the larger culture, or they can manage a subculture of their own design. With all the knowledge available about human resources management, managers or executives who fly by the seat of their pants are no longer acceptable.

The Leader's Role in Culture Change

Changing an organization's culture is an option to be selected only after a thorough analysis of the existing culture. Before rushing in with changes, you must understand the culture as it exists and be clear about where you want it to go.

In a large organization, shifting the culture is like turning a battleship. The captain should plan well in advance, have ample power, have enough time and space, and forget about turning it on a dime. Turning around smaller organizations is like turning a cruiser; the principles are the same, but the time frame is shorter. Here are some reasons you might consider undertaking a culture shift:

- You are a new CEO brought in to fix a crumbling company. You will need to take some exceptional risks to succeed.
- You are the responsible leader in a merger or acquisition. The two cultures are very different and you need to choose one for the merged companies.
- You are a middle manager in a large organization and the team you are taking over is out of step with the direction of the company.
- You are a leader in the midst of a personal transformation. You believe deeply that you can have a more effective organization and create a happier, healthier worklife for everyone by going all-out for a collaborative environment, open communication, and participative management.
- The new strategic plan you have spent months developing cannot be implemented by the organization, given its current culture, and you and your executive team are committed to this plan.

You may have other reasons to embark on a culture change, but they ought to be at least as good as these, and you should be a real believer in the new culture you want to install. Ways to go about making a culture change can be found throughout this book. In a large organization, culture change is a massive project and you would be wise to consider bringing in a knowledgeable outside person to assist you.

The Basics of Culture Diagnosis

Much of the material in the topics that follow is by permission of Len Korot, Ph.D., Professor of Behavioral Science, School of Business and Management, Pepperdine University. His continuing research into organizational culture is providing new insights for corporate executives.

In the field of organizational development, little agreement is found on the precise definition of culture, and even less on how to measure it. Writers and researchers brings their biases to the subject. This is the bias that we share with Len Korot: organizational culture is an excellent framework for illuminating all of organizational behavior.

Even though a manager's analysis of culture may not pass rigorous scientific examination, when done with reasonable application and care, it can lead to an understanding of what makes an organization tick. Armed with this insight, managers know what part of the organization to tweak to improve overall effectiveness.

At the beginning of this chapter, culture was defined as "the shared behaviors, norms, values, and assumptions that knit an organization together." To analyze your culture you must see what is taking place in each of these areas.

Looking at Dr. Korot's Organizational Culture Iceberg illustration on the following page, you can see that three of the areas of exploration — Artifacts, Perceptions, and Daily Beliefs — are either visible or can become visible by asking direct questions. They are the tip of the iceberg. They provide some insights that are helpful in understanding culture.

The deeper basis of a culture is invisible and less easy to determine, however. As shown, it consists of the Values and Driving Beliefs held by the key members of the organization. They are more difficult to diagnose because they do not come to light in response to direct questions.

The Organizational Culture Iceberg

How do people act?

Artifacts: Those tangible aspects of culture that one sees, hears, or feels when observing an organization.

What do people say?

Perceptions: The way people describe how a wide range of activities is accomplished.

How is the game played?

Daily Beliefs: The day-to-day operational choices that influence individual behavior on the job. Often called norms, standards, or rules.

What is the management philosophy?

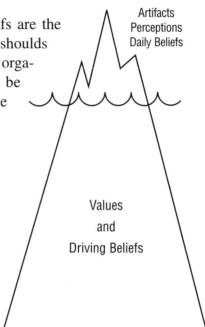

Artifacts
Perceptions
Daily Beliefs

Values
and
Driving Beliefs

Values: Underlying the daily beliefs are the unstated rights and wrongs, the shoulds and should-nots that establish the organizational identity. This could be expressed as goals, ideals, people concepts, "sins," or levels of aggressiveness.

What are the basic assumptions held by the key players?

Driving Beliefs: The core perceptions formed in early childhood are largely outside of consciousness. Illuminating these basic assumptions is the most difficult and most essential task in diagnosing organizational culture.

To begin your own culture analysis, follow the procedure outlined below.

Complete the Culture Profile

Warning: Doing a cultural analysis may be hazardous to your financial health! You will be discussing issues that can cause organizational turmoil if you do the analysis without permission of top officers. Always have agreement at key levels about the long-range benefits of examining the culture before you begin.

Hand out the Korot Organizational Culture Profile (found at the end of this chapter) to key members of the organization and ask them to complete and return it to you. Assure everyone of anonymity so they can respond honestly. If you are trying to determine the culture of a small company, or a small group within a larger organization, you may wish to include in your survey everyone from the top leader down.

In a larger company analysis, you should always survey the top management team as one group. Then, you can survey other levels of management in separate groups. If you can include segments of line workers, you will round out the picture and give yourself an opportunity to compare responses across groups. Tabulate responses by averaging answers to each question, then use a blank form to record them. Draw lines from one circled number to another to get a profile of the group. Also, note the range of responses — this will tell you whether people view the culture in much the same way or very differently. If you uncover some disparity between groups, this will provide important information to use in a step that follows.

The Culture Profile also will give you perceptions about how the organization handles matters pertaining to its internal environment and how it responds to its external environment. This distinction is important because in managing culture change, an organization must first learn to function smoothly internally to respond appropriately to external factors. The Culture Profile measures internal factors in questions D, E, F, J, K, L, M, N, O. It measures external factors in questions A, C, H. Questions B, G, I, P have elements of both internal and external. You can graph the internal and external responses on the summary form, in addition to the overall profile.

Remember, the completed Culture Profile will tell you how your organization perceives itself, not what constitutes the essential culture. For this insight you need to do additional work.

Conduct an Artifacts Audit

While the Culture Profile is in process, walk around and make note of things you see that will identify some of the visible aspects of the culture. Is there a special parking area for management, or is the space open to everyone? Are managers and others segregated in the lunchroom? How is the physical working area allocated? What are the accepted ways of decorating one's own space? What kind of art is used in the facility? What is the dress standard? You will find a variety of other artifacts to add to your list. Examining these will give you some clues about the next level of exploration.

Analyze the "Daily Beliefs" System

Daily beliefs or norms get started when people come together and bring with them, or form, certain expectations regarding one another's behavior. Every culture has its way of doing things that influences its members. When someone takes a position on an issue and then everyone "buys in," a norm is taking shape. In the formative period of an organization many such events arise.

Once established, these tacit understandings form the basis for daily activities. Norms stay around because they work, and members of the culture feel comfortable with them. Some norms you might see:

- The company expects employees to arrive on time (or late or early).
- Employees do not openly criticize the boss (or, open discussion of all issues is the way we do it).
- Reward your friends.
- Don't be a star.
- Believe the numbers.

Understanding the norms is critical in culture analysis because an employee very quickly can become an outsider, or see plans defeated, by defying the daily belief system.

Examine Values and Driving Beliefs

Now the more difficult part begins, because you are working with that part of the Cultural Iceberg below the water line and not available for easy viewing. Your inquiry focuses on two areas — Values and Driving Beliefs.

Values become understandable in a variety of ways. Sometimes corporate slogans such as, "Respect for the Individual," "Do it Right," and "Universal Service" point the way. Heroes and heroines personify values. Stories about these figures may highlight the values or essential philosophy of the organization. You can hear the values being expressed when members are concerned about what will happen as figures who embody the spirit of the company depart.

Rituals are an expression of cultural values. Observing a work unit in process is often like observing a well-choreographed dance. In one organization, the Friday afternoon beer party is where many of the problems get handled. Rituals anchor some aspects of a culture, and how to use or alter them makes for an interesting management challenge. Ceremonies are displays of organizational values. Christmas parties, retreats, and annual get-togethers are sure to bring out all the the flags and speeches that give valuable cultural insights.

Storytellers and "corporate characters" are important clues to a culture, too. They form a continuity between old and emerging values. They either retell old tales or become the subject of the stories. Values permeate all levels of the organization and those promulgated at the top influence the entire culture.

Driving beliefs are the very essence of organizational culture. They are the tacit assumptions the organization makes about itself, others, and the world in which it functions. One important basic belief, below the surface in every organization, is about the nature of humankind. A possible view is: given a responsive environment, humans are innately self-motivated, seek responsibility and challenge, and are capable of continual growth and development. A completely opposite view is: humans must be coerced to accomplish, are essentially noncreative, avoid responsibility, and their approach to life is fixed and virtually unalterable. Which of these views is held will drive everything that involves people in the organization. Having an accurate fix on this driving belief is essential to cultural understanding.

Another assumption regards truth. Does the belief assume truth is revealed by an authority or determined by a process of personal testing? The former sets the stage for authoritarian leadership.

What about beliefs regarding human relationships? What is the "right" way for people to relate to each other? Is life cooperative or competitive? Is it individualistic or group collaborative? Which belief predominates will determine the probability of participative management thriving.

Is the basic belief that human beings can master the environment, or that they should attempt to harmonize with the environment? How this belief is held determines a whole range of organizational dynamics. These and other driving beliefs are at the very core of organizational behavior, yet they are not easy to see or analyze. Just as these assumptions guide the behavior of each of us, so they guide the behavior of organizations. While values, artifacts, and perceptions form parts of a culture, driving beliefs determine how it operates when the chips are down.

Start Asking Questions

This part of your cultural analysis will bring to light the values and driving beliefs of your organization. Assemble the people who responded to the Korot Organizational Culture Profile. Work with fewer than ten at a time. This may be the complete group or representative members. In a large organization work separately with the several groups you surveyed.

If individual responses to the survey were widely scattered, you can begin to question why focus seems to be missing in the company. This may be due to a brief history, lack of objectives, or crisis management. Reaching a joint understanding of the assumptions that led to a lack of cohesiveness can help you understand how to establish a culture to answer your needs.

More often, the responses to the survey cluster around one number, with an occasional person holding a different view. Begin examining those items that measure how the organization handles its internal environment. Talk about the values and driving beliefs that underlie your perceptions of how the organization functions. (While you are guiding this discussion don't forget to be a process-watcher. How the group handles the discussion yields additional clues to the culture).

As an example, suppose you are tracking item E: Autonomy versus Requirement for Control, and your average group score was 3. As you explore how this manifests itself, you uncover a number of managerial behaviors that support your perceptions. Perhaps the artifacts, such as a number of executive privileges, add to the picture. What driving belief underlies this? Probably it's the one about the nature of humankind. Somehow, in our example, key leaders have a fundamental belief that they need to control people, that workers are essentially noncreative and avoid responsibility and challenge. Talk about this ticklish subject some, and see if what you have really is a pervasive belief.

Now look at item M: Organizational Structure. This is essentially another way of looking at the same issue E does. Chances are the scores you agree on for E and M will be similar, because the same basic assumption drives both.

Other driving beliefs are about the nature of truth, the nature of human relationships, the nature of time, and the organization's relationship to its environment. You can look for one or more basic assumptions behind the collective response to each question in the Culture Profile. When your discussion ends (it may take several meetings) you will know whether your organization is culturally defined as Traditional Management or as New Management, and perhaps to what degree. With that knowledge, you will be able to decide whether your culture is optimally effective for dealing with the demands of your external environment and the needs of your people, or if it needs some fixing.

Korot Organizational Culture Profile

For each of the following cultural characteristics, circle the number on the continuum from 1 to 9 which you feel best describes your organization.

A. Innovation and Risk Taking

1   2   3   4   5   6   7   8   9

1 = Emphasis on stability; little willingness to innovate or take risks.

9 = Strong commitment to innovation and risk taking.

B. Concern About Quality in Products and Services

1   2   3   4   5   6   7   8   9

1 = Low concern about quality; company is willing to accept "average" as its standard.

9 = High concern about quality; "superior" is the only acceptable standard.

C. Responsiveness to Customer Needs

1   2   3   4   5   6   7   8   9

1 = Low sensitivity to customer satisfaction; concern about the customer is only given lip service.

9 = Concern about the customer is part of the daily consciousness of employees throughout the organization.

D. Responsiveness to Employee Needs

1   2   3   4   5   6   7   8   9

1 = Employees are seen as objects to be used to meet top management's goals; personnel programs concentrate on basic security needs.

9 = Management invests significant resources in personnel programs that encourage personal growth and development.

E. Autonomy versus Requirement for Control

       1   2   3   4   5   6   7   8   9

1 = Organization is dominated by management's need for control. Very little room for employee initiative, self-direction, and participation in policy decisions that affect their work.

9 = High ability for both individuals and groups to exercise initiative and self-direction in carrying out their work and in making policy decisions about their work.

F. Systems of Incentives

       1   2   3   4   5   6   7   8   9

1 = Seniority and loyalty are most highly rewarded; no meaningful incentives for exceptional performance.

9 = Broad commitment throughout the organization to recognizing and rewarding exceptional performance.

G. Time Orientation and View of Change

       1   2   3   4   5   6   7   8   9

1 = Orientation is almost always historical; reference point is "We have always done it this way — why change?"

9 = Orientation is future driven; reference point is "What are the future pay-offs? Why not change?"

H. Environmental Scanning

       1   2   3   4   5   6   7   8   9

1 = Organization ignores or gives minimal attention to changes in the external environment; almost no investment in time and resources in re-examining strategic and marketing assumptions.

9 = Heavy and continual investment in scanning the external environment and in testing strategic and marketing assumptions.

I. Standardization

1   2   3   4   5   6   7   8   9

1 = Emphasis is strict adherence to documented administrative policies and procedures. It is virtually impossible to change policies for monitoring and measuring performance.

9 = Emphasis is on flexibility in dealing with day-to-day operating problems. Systems for monitoring and measuring performance are easily modified and are designed to facilitate problem solving.

J. Approach to the Capture, Analysis, and Transfer of Information

1   2   3   4   5   6   7   8   9

1 = Access to and use of key financial and operational information is restricted to upper management.

9 = Access to and use of key information is broadly available throughout the organization.

K. Company Cohesiveness

1   2   3   4   5   6   7   8   9

1 = Company is stratified and disconnected; communication and collaboration among subunits is weak or nonexistent.

9 = Company is cohesive and connected; communication and collaboration among subunits is high.

L. Leadership and Vision

1   2   3   4   5   6   7   8   9

1 = Company vision and future direction is neither visible nor understood throughout the organization.

9 = There is a clear company vision and sense of direction, visible and understood throughout the organization.

M. Organizational Structure

　　　　　1　2　3　4　5　6　7　8　9

1 = Organization is highly structured; responsibilities are rigidly defined and movement of people within the organization is infrequent.

9 = Organization is loosely defined; mobility within the company is high and responsibilities are fluid and shaped by changing conditions.

N. Collaboration in Problem Solving

　　　　　1　2　3　4　5　6　7　8　9

1 = Individuals work on their own; group involvement in problem solving is minimal; collaboration is virtually nonexistent.

9 = Organization is highly collaborative at all levels; members seek each other out to assist in problem solving.

O. Timeliness of Decision Making

　　　　　1　2　3　4　5　6　7　8　9

1 = Decision making is slow; generation of required data takes large amounts of time and the data is continually re-examined.

9 = Decisions are reached rapidly; a sense of appropriate urgency is constantly felt.

P. Strategic Planning Process

　　　　　1　2　3　4　5　6　7　8　9

1 = Strategic planning is concentrated at the top; little effort is made to get the organization as a whole to "own" strategic goals.

9 = Strategic planning involves a cross section of the organization; strong effort is made to develop broad ownership of strategic goals by all employees.

Additional Information

Books

Culture.com: Building Corporate Culture in the Connected Workplace, Peg C. Neuhauser et al, John Wiley & Sons, 2000. Tackles the question of how to create a corporate culture in the new dotcom business strategy.

The Corporate Culture Survival Guide, Edgar Schein, Jossey-Bass, 1999. Explains culture as "the essence" of the company and illustrates how a company's culture can be deliberately created or changed.

Act Like an Owner: Building an Ownership Culture, Robert M. Blonchek and Martin F. O'Neill, John Wiley & Sons, 1999. An action guide to building a culture of employee ownership within an organization.

Corporate Culture and Change, (pamphlet) Melissa A. Berman, editor, The Conference Board, 1986. A report for top management.

Gaining Control of the Corporate Culture, Ralph H. Kilmann et al, Jossey-Bass, 1985. A selection of articles by authorities in the field. Provides a multitude of views on the subject.

Organizational Culture, Peter J. Frost et al, Sage Publications, 1985. This is a work by and for scholars.

Corporate Cultures, Terrence E. Deal and Allen A. Kennedy, Addison-Wesley, 1982. This was the first major work on the subject. It makes a case for strong cultures.

How to Interpret the Test to Chapter 10

If you answered "Yes" to all ten, move to the head of the class.

Chapter 11

How Do You Rate as a Multicultural Manager?

To get an idea of how sensitive you are to current multicultural issues and trends, assign a "Yes" or "No" to each of the following statements and then check your answers at the end of this chapter.

	Yes	No
1. White males are the dominant group in the U.S. workforce.	☐	☐
2. In the 21st Century, 75% of those entering the workforce will be minorities and women.	☐	☐
3. The Business Council for International Understanding estimates that international personnel who go abroad without cross-cultural preparation have a failure rate ranging from 33%–66%, in contrast to less than 2% of those who have had training.	☐	☐
4. People are people, and managing them today is very much as it was twenty years ago.	☐	☐
5. European business managers have a great deal more international experience than their American counterparts.	☐	☐
6. Stereotypes of people from other cultures do not interfere with managing a diverse workforce.	☐	☐
7. Americans are often intolerant of and have a tendency to think of people from other cultures as inferior.	☐	☐
8. Hiring the person best qualified for a position is a practice honored in all cultures.	☐	☐
9. The type of awareness and sensitivity advocated in other chapters of this book serve the manager well in cross-cultural interactions.	☐	☐
10. Even though some cultures tend toward individualism, the new multicultural manager will increasingly emphasize some form of team approach in the workplace.	☐	☐

Chapter 11

Becoming Multicultural

The Shrinking Globe

From its beginning, the United States was a "melting pot" of peoples and cultures, primarily of European stock. Each wave of English, German, Irish, French, and Italian immigrants brought with it new and distinctive ways that were adapted, adopted, transformed, and homogenized so that in a generation or two national origins became blurred. Conformity was expected and eventually people learned to act in "the American way," making it possible to get readings on how people were going to behave in a given situation. In a typical domestic company, doing business with and through people was relatively straightforward.

Again, America is being transformed by a new wave of immigrants, but today's immigrants are, for the most part, from Asia, Latin America, and the Middle East. The "melting pot" has been replaced with a "tossed salad" society, where cultural elements are all mixed together but retain many of their original characteristics.

This resistance to enculturation poses new challenges to management, while the abundant talent and work-hard ethic of the new Americans changes and enriches our workplace and all of society.

Adding more challenges to management is the increasingly global nature of business. Hardly any business is purely domestic today. Many engage in direct trade or provide services overseas. Components of goods manufactured locally are often from other countries, or locally owned plants may be situated offshore. It's not unusual to have an American management team operating a plant in Mexico that is financed by Japan. Now, the rapid expansion of other economies and the opening of borders, particularly in the European Economic Community, bring opportunities for internationalization of even more U.S. businesses. Managers who lack the flexibility to adapt will be pushed aside by others who are more culturally savvy and resilient.

This is not to say that American managers are the only ones who face the globalization dilemma. Europeans, Asians, Africans, Latin Americans — people of all countries — are affected by a shrinking globe. While managers in other countries may have the advantage of speaking more than one language and are sometimes more experienced international travelers, they, too, confess similar naivete in dealing with other cultures. In fact, expressions of chauvinism, ethnocentrism (cultural superiority), insensitivity, and resistance to cultural mixing are frequently more observable abroad than in the United States.

The New Cosmopolitan Manager

Today we are all global citizens and cosmopolitan managers must think and act in more culturally-sensitive lives. Such individuals manage change and differences in their own life, are willing to alter personal attitudes and perceptions, and can cope with people who have backgrounds quite different from their own.

The new cosmopolitan managers are conceptualizers who think in global rather than local terms. They have the mind of the strategist — the ability to stand apart from any situation and see all the diverse interactions as part of one huge panorama, not as separate events — and they can see how tweaking one part of the system may affect all the others. In dealing with people, this ability allows them to always make the intervention that is appropriate to the situation, rather than reacting from the narrow perspective created by their own cultural blinders.

The cosmopolitan manager understands that some human characteristics have always been universal, but a unique world culture is emerging and leaders must be in the vanguard of change.

Becoming the New Cosmopolitan Manager

Each person's perceptions and behaviors are guided by cultural assumptions. Becoming multicultural requires you to recognize that values, ethics, and even "common sense" are transient and vary according to cultural circumstances.

Human existence is inherently multicultural — we live together on the planet, but with vast cultural differences. To coexist, we emphasize our similarities, but never really deal with our differences. We build spells around our own culture that will not permit us to acknowledge or accept the validity of other cultural perspectives. In this way we brush up against each other but never really embrace.

The new cosmopolitanism calls for an attitude of inquiry and a willingness to suspend judgment when dealing with the complexity of cultural issues. It means consciously moving from ethnocentricity to being geocentric (having a world view).

The changes required of the manager becoming multicultural are not much different from those advocated in earlier chapters of this book. The process is centered in self-awareness, particularly bringing into consciousness those basic beliefs that were learned in childhood, that continue to guide your perceptions of, and behavior toward, other cultures.

The first step toward understanding another culture is to understand your own. You can't leave home without your frame of reference and value system, nor should you. But if you really want to understand what's going on and deal effectively with a foreign situation or a multicultural workforce at home, you need to understand your own assumptions and how different they are from the rest of the world's. With this clarity, you can allow yourself to park your realities and enter those of another. When you are able to do this at will, being multicultural is possible. Understanding oneself and understanding others are closely-related processes; to do one you must start with the other.

Becoming aware means switching from automatic to manual — noticing what is happening in your daily thoughts and actions, then searching your memory for the voice that first told you to think or behave that way. When you can identify where you first learned something (for example, a particular prejudice), you begin to understand that your reality is a point of view created for you and not necessarily the only reality or perspective. Over time you can come to acknowledge alternative realities, becoming comfortable in a multitude of cultures. This is a complex and difficult process, not one you can accomplish overnight. While some people do have an instant spiritual transformation, usually this follows a long period of inner searching. Though few attempt it, making it to the exalted level where alternate realities are perceived is within reach of everyone.

The following ideas about cross-cultural managing may give you additional insights. The last part of this chapter describes individual and group experiences that will begin your transformation to a cosmopolite.

- To fully understand another culture, you need to learn the language. By getting inside the language you can experience the values and feel the cultural nuances.

- What this chapter describes is the general intellectual and psychological orientation of anyone who is managing a diverse workforce at home or abroad. Once your personal change process is underway, you are ready to begin your in-depth study of the culture(s) with which you are involved.

- A key to cross-cultural understanding is building relationships over time. The usual American businessperson's orientation is to deal with facts only and arrive at decisions quickly. Learn to take your time with people of another culture; let them set the pace rather than following your own impulses.

- Whenever you hear yourself saying about people from another culture, "They are really no different from the folks back home; they are just like I am," be aware that you are coming from your own single-world context. Acknowledging and dealing with differences is the cosmopolitan way.

- When you deal with a diverse domestic workforce, be sure the rules and standards don't assume a white male group. What may have once been homogeneity has been replaced with diversity.

- You were probably taught to manage people equally. Remember that being "equal" does not mean everyone is the same. Also, be aware that equality and equal treatment is not the norm in some other cultures.

- Everyone from every background, needs to be heard if the organization is to succeed. The manager's responsibility is to make sure that everyone is an "insider."

- The same carrot doesn't work for everyone. Watch when you give public recognition, establish standards of pay for performance, and handle many other common organizational acts that were, but may no longer be, "the American way."

- Organizations should not compromise their standards to accommodate cultural differences. It would be demeaning to everyone. Competence is gender and race neutral.

- Human nature, as we conceive it, may not be human nature at all, but complex learned behavior. Anything learned can be unlearned or reoriented.

- When people have been taught how to learn in a certain way, learning in another way is extremely difficult. Consider this when you design a training program for a diverse workforce.

- Becoming multicultural means you may have to alter your habits, attitudes, values, tastes, relationships, or sources of satisfaction.

- Whatever else is said, absolutely no substitute exists for extensive immersion in another culture. Taking a ten-country tour with brief stop overs won't do it.

- Watch that you don't search for rules instead of developing understanding. In a foreign place, looking, listening, and having the right attitude are more important than being able to speak the language or knowing the rules.

- Don't assume that those from another culture who speak English understand what you are saying, and don't assume because you speak a language that you understand the culture.

- Learn to see differences as opportunities rather than constraints.

You have probably discovered by now that the same process that will lead you to becoming a team player, collaborative manager, open communicator, and a developer of people is the one that will lead you to becoming a multicultural person. Whichever avenue of personal transformation you take, the outcome will include all of these facets.

The "As If" Method: A Personal Strategy

To make the transition from parochial thinking to geocentric, first do a variety of reading about culture, then mentally chew on the concepts, attempting to get a complete cognitive picture of what may be required to reframe your beliefs. While your mind may tell you that being able to perceive alternate realities is an idea with great possibilities, your own single-level cultural beliefs may not let this new concept push its way through into total acceptance. A huge gap separates intellectual understanding and real acceptance.

You can start closing this gap through "as if" behavior. Tell yourself that you are going to think and behave as if these new concepts are fully a part of you — that you are going to be an experimenter in the new idea. For example, in a foreign country you might be watching a ritual that your cultural background tells you is amusing or weird. Rather than walk away, join that ritual as a participant to the extent that you are able, experiencing whatever is happening from the perspective of that culture. Rather than simply observing the culture, attempt to be in it. Respond to the experience not just in a cerebral way, but in a visceral way as well. With your entire being in the process, you will get the full impact of another reality and perhaps make it an acceptable part of your own reality as well. In this way you move into new worlds.

This is not easy, and something magical may not happen with every attempt, but if you continue to explore other realities with all your senses, your belief system will begin to expand and change.

Cross-Cultural Experiences at Home

If you are seriously interested in moving toward global consciousness, you can undertake a variety of experiences. Remember that the purpose of all your effort is to foster awareness. Pay attention to how your own cultural perspective takes over, and make a conscious effort to learn new ways. Then make the new perspectives part of the multicultural person you are becoming.

- Analyze a prejudice you hold. How did it develop? What function does it serve now? How can you go about setting it aside? How will eliminating this prejudice alter your world view? Write a letter to yourself as you go through this analysis and reread it whenever you feel the need.

- Interview someone who has lived and worked overseas. What obstacles did he or she face? What personal skills were necessary to be successful abroad? What did this person learn about cultural blocks that can give you insights into your own?

- Take a foreign trip right here in the United States. Plan an immersion experience of several days in an ethnic neighborhood in your own city or in one of the major U.S. cities. Really live in the community, shopping, eating in local restaurants, talking with people. Try to get as deeply involved as possible. At the end of each day make notes of your experiences. If you can take this immersion trip at the same time as several of your associates (but not together), comparing notes and feelings at the end will enhance the learning.

- Make friends with new immigrants, foreign students, or managers from another culture. Let them share their experiences as foreigners coming to the United States. How did they view Americans? How did their cultural blocks inhibit their becoming comfortable in the United States culture? What can you learn and use from their transitions?

- Check the local paper for different cultural festivities and plan to attend several. It could be a celebration such as Cinco de Mayo, an art show, or an annual parade. Really get involved by entering into the activities, eating the food, and talking with people about the history. Notice your reactions, particularly what you reject.

- Throw a cross-cultural party at work. Have all participants bring food to share from their culture. Discuss the origins of the food and have fun together.

Cross-Cultural Experiences Abroad

Plan to take your next vacation outside the United States, and confine it to one country. In addition to the usual fun you have, plan to make this trip one that will broaden your understanding of the culture. Arrange to travel on your own, not with a tour. Make all the reservations yourself or be an active partner with your travel agent. Before you go, read literature from the country you plan to visit, particularly novels and plays. When you arrive at your destination, try some of these suggestions for cultural enrichment.

- Be adventurous. Go into nontourist restaurants and do things off the beaten track.

- Get lost and find your way back to the hotel. See what's behind some of the doors you pass.

- Let go of your inhibitions and experience fully what being in another world is like.

- Meet the children. Go to a park and watch them play. Get involved and speak with them. Children will accept you readily and allow you to experiment with their language without embarrassing you. Deep insights into the culture are available through observing children's activities.

- Watch movies made within the country.

- Read some periodicals. If you don't speak the local language, search out English-language editions of local papers and magazines.

If you do enough of these kinds of things, you will eventually find that your cultural horizons are greatly expanded. You will have a powerful new frame of reference certain to serve you well in managing people and in enjoying your everyday life.

Additional Information

Books

Breaking Through Culture Shock: What You Need to Succeed in International Business, Elisabeth Marx, Nicholas Brealey, 1999. Examines the phenomenon of culture shock and offers coping strategies.

Experiencing International Management, PWS-Kent Publishing Company, 1989. Experiential learning exercises and activities that can be used in training international managers.

Tomorrow's Global Executive, Henry Ferguson, Dow Jones-Irwin, 1988. For the seasoned executive facing a new world of global competition.

Going International, Lennie Copeland and Lewis Griggs, Random House, 1985. A guidebook for employees and families living abroad and international travelers.

Managing Cultural Differences, Philip R. Harris and Robert T. Moran, Gulf Publishing Company, 1979. Performance strategies for the global manager.

Resources

If you would like to speak with Phyllis Herrin, Ph.D., president of Personnel Consulting Group, Inc. regarding her work in nonsexist language, women's issues, and managing diversity, contact The Oasis Press.

How to Interpret the Test for Chapter 11

Check your answers:

1. No. They represent only forty-six percent of the current workforce.

2. Yes.

3. Yes.

4. No. In times of dramatic change, the way you managed last year may be out-moded today.

5. Yes, Europeans cross borders regularly, have new cultural experiences often, and may speak several languages. Americans are much more isolated. Europeans, however, are not necessarily more sensitive to cultural differences.

6. No. Your stereotypes usually derive from your own cultural biases and may tend to mislead in a diverse environment. Unfounded stereotypes must be replaced with understanding and sensitivity to the nuances of other cultures.

7. Yes. Note, however, that most other cultures are similarly chauvinistic.

8. No. Family, friendships, and other considerations often take precedence in other cultures.

9. Yes. Personal awareness and sensitivity is a key attribute in cross-cultural management.

10. Yes, but multicultural team building gets more tricky.

Chapter 12

The Management Challenge in a Turbulent World

Anti-Change Forces

Understanding Resistance to Change

Concepts for Handling Personal Change

Concepts for Becoming a Leader of Change

Change Rating

For a change, test yourself on your adaptability to change. See the discussion of these questions on the last page of this chapter.

	Yes	No
1. Thinking carefully about the effect on individuals and groups of any changes, even of minor rules, is important.	☐	☐
2. Change should be instituted through a carefully worded company directive.	☐	☐
3 Change is exciting for most people.	☐	☐
4. Small work units are more effective than large ones.	☐	☐
5. People today are pretty much the same as they were ten or fifteen years ago.	☐	☐
6. Experience is the best teacher.	☐	☐
7. The more information employees receive about planned change, the less the possibility of resistance.	☐	☐
8. Long-range planning facilitates change.	☐	☐
9. Rigid organizational structures inhibit change.	☐	☐
10. Change should be planned secretly, then pushed through rapidly before anyone is aware.	☐	☐

Chapter 12

Changing

This new world will be more human and humane. It will explore and develop the richness and capacities of the human mind and spirit. It will produce individuals who are more integrated and whole. It will be a world that prizes the individual person — a test of our resources. It will be a more natural world, with a renewed love and respect for nature. It will develop a more human science, based on new and less rigid concepts. Its technology will be aimed at the enhancing, rather than the exploitation, of persons and nature. It will release creativity as individuals sense their power, their capacities, their freedom.

Carl R. Rogers
A Way of Being

The Management Challenge in a Turbulent World

It's almost a cliché to say we live in an era of unprecedented uncertainty. Peter Vail[4] characterizes the times as permanent white water. The world social order is changing at a dizzying pace, no rules guide global business, and the domestic business environment is so chaotic that experience may

---

4. Peter Vail, *Managing as a Performing Art* (San Francisco: Jossey-Bass, 1989), p. 2.

now be the worst teacher. Yet it is in this extraordinary setting that you must manage your own life and the destiny of your organization.

Ubiquitous change is now a basic reality of organizational life and no firm is immune to the process. As a manager your choices are: plan extensively and attempt to use change to your advantage or do nothing, muddle along, and risk being overwhelmed by changing conditions. The white water analogy is worth examining. In a raging stream the inclination is to grab for a firm branch on shore, to anchor yourself in something stable that won't give way. But the permanent white water of today has no shoreline, so the only option is to go with the flow. This is a way of viewing the new situation and understanding that survival really offers no alternatives.

Anti-Change Forces

Most managers and executives view themselves as readily accepting of change. They cite how easily they moved across the country to accept a new position, or the various job changes they have made. But too often, when challenged with a new situation in their business, or when working on a case history involving organizational change, they react with proven formulas rather than apply creative options that come from viewing the new situation in an equally new way.

Making the switch from being change resistant to being open to change is very difficult in contemporary America; little in our daily experience encourages creativity. We have become expert at ignoring the long-range in favor of short-term results when one of the best ways to deal with a changing world is to have a longer-range vision. The negative effects of this can be seen everywhere: Our refusal to recast education in our primary schools is disastrous in a turbulent world; our fixation on quarterly results keeps us from developing long-range plans; our proclivity for discouraging risk-taking in the organization is a veneration of the status quo.

Understanding Resistance to Change

Fear of the unknown is frightening to everyone. Often, people will prolong a disastrous relationship because of fear of what it may be like to be alone; some will stay in an unsatisfying job for fear of the risk involved in change. For many, the certainty of misery is preferable to the misery of uncertainty.

Ida Fisher,[5] described the stages of grief in response to the death of a loved one. These stages are applicable to any ending of a psychologically important event. Change is such an ending. It's a loss of the known, then moving into the unknown while letting go of various fixities in our lives.

The stages an individual goes through in the face of major change are:

- Denial. In this first stage people reject the impending or occurring change. They may refuse to even acknowledge the change, no matter how obvious. In organizations, they often dig in their heels, adamantly refusing to participate — almost as if the change is not taking place. In times of turbulence, some people hole up, playing ostrich, believing that if they don't look the change won't occur.

- Numbness. Once the inevitable becomes clear, a mild state of shock may set in. People will respond to the change edict, but in a robot-like fashion, contributing little that is not mechanical.

- Disorganization. Out of the old, but not yet into the new, many become disoriented, forgetful, confused. This is a particularly difficult period in organizational change because everyone is needed to pitch in, but many are not up to the requirement.

- Anger. In this stage, heads are clear and the full impact of the change sets in. With this comes anger and feelings of being treated unfairly. This stage can be particularly destructive and may even lead to sabotage of the change process.

- Acceptance. In the final stage, things come together, the inevitable is totally clear, and people can start working together to facilitate the new way.

When you understand the complex human dynamics in the change process, you can be observant and accepting of yourself as you experience these various stages. As a leader in organizational change, you can design the process so it is not too precipitous, includes empathy for people, and allows for discussion at all stages so the changes can take place without excessive trauma.

Concepts for Handling Personal Change

This entire book is about change, both personal and organizational. Here we focus on change as a process and review and augment those specific

---

5. Ida Fisher and Byron Lane, *The Widow's Guide to Life* (New York: Prentice-Hall, 1981), pp. 5–6.

beliefs and behaviors that will put you into the flow of change, making you an agent for change in others.

Switching the locus of your personal security from dependence on the external environment to dependence upon yourself is the first and most important step in becoming a whitewater navigator. This is simply another aspect of the theme that runs throughout this book. You alone are responsible for how your life fares, and you can make the necessary choices. This means doing your inner work, as elsewhere described in this book. Once you realize that whatever certainties you need for stability in a turbulent world reside inside you already, and you love and accept yourself for who you are, then you will always remain afloat in the white water. Some concepts that will aid you in becoming comfortable with change are:

- Have a proactive approach to change, and use it as a source of advantage.

- Significant change can occur only when you are willing to modify your belief about how things ought to be and then develop a commitment to new methods and ideas.

- Consider living with paradox. Not everything needs to make sense.

- Avoid being defensive when someone challenges your cherished views.

- Create a personal vision. Get a clear picture of who you are and where you are going. The more clear this picture becomes, the more stabilizing it will be for you in the changing environment.

Concepts for Becoming a Leader of Change

Being a leader in organizational change requires that you first be a person who thrives on change, tolerates a high level of ambiguity, and keeps a clear head and open heart in the midst of chaos. Only from this position can you become an effective leader who is an agent for change.

Once clear personally, the leader of change becomes a visionary. Seeing and articulating the "big picture" is the hallmark of the effective manager or executive. The way to stabilize an organization internally, in the midst of chaotic change, is to have a vision of the future backed up with a strategic plan in which everyone has ownership. Implementation of the plan is the marching order and, in this way, everyone has clarity even when all around there may be turmoil.

If you would like to try creating a vision for your organization, write an article for your favorite business publication. Describe your organization five years from now and the part you will play in the transformation. Use a free-flowing style as you might for a novel.

In addition to promoting the vision, as leader/change-agent you may want to adopt these characteristics, beliefs, or styles:

- Be a courageous risk-taker. Only those willing to create something different can lead in a time of uncertainty.

- Encourage constant testing of the vision, then adapt the vision to meet the changing world.

- Have a deep belief in people.

- Take the attitude that conflict is healthy and allow people of goodwill to see their disparate views as material for personal and organizational growth.

- Manage by anticipation rather than crisis. When people see where they are headed they are less likely to resist change.

- Make changes only in a setting of participatory democracy. Never order people to change. People will support what they helped create.

- Show people how a proposed change will help them. If it includes no benefit for them, don't institute the change.

- Open up all the communication channels. Nothing kills off a plan for change faster than the rumor mill. Anything you leave unsaid will be filled in with a rumor.

Remember that changing even one little rule in the smallest company has repercussions for someone. The unthinking manager gets resistance; the change-agent manager gets support.

Additional Information

Books

Managing People Is Like Herding Cats, Warren G. Bennis, Executive Excellence, 1999. Cats, of course, won't be herded. This book details the qualities that successful leaders must have as they move towards change.

10 Good reasons Why People Resist Change: And Practical Strategies that Win the Day, James O.B. Keener, Grand River Publishing, 1999. Gets to the heart of successfully managing change.

Sacred Cows Make the Best Burgers: Developing Change-Ready People and Organizations, Robert Kriegel, Warner Books, 1997. Shows how organizations can kill off the sacred cows that are crippling them.

Taking Charge of Change, Douglas K. Smith, Perseus Press, 1997. Diagnostic tools to assess needs for change and the toolkit to implement the changes.

Leading Change, James O'Toole, Jossey-Bass, 1995. How change agents can gain commitment from their people.

Second to None, Charles Garfield, Business One Irwin, 1992. The stories of the companies who are changing the way business is done in the nineties.

New Traditions in Business, John Renesch, editor, Sterling and Stone, 1991. Visionary business leaders describe the transformational changes underway.

The Rapids of Change, Robert Theobold, Knowledge Systems, Inc., 1987. Answers the question, "How can individuals make a difference today?"

Thriving on Chaos, Tom Peters, Knopf, 1987. Everything you need to watch out for in a whitewater world.

On Becoming a Person, Carl R. Rogers, The Riverside Press, 1961. An important seminal work on personal change by one of the foremost psychologists of the twentieth century.

How to Interpret the Test for Chapter 12

People who deal extensively with organizational and individual change would answer this way:

1. Yes. Change is frightening for most people.

2. No. This is a way to get into real trouble. See the recommendations in this chapter.

3. No. See 1 above.

4. Yes. Smaller units make for higher visibility and greater comfort.

5. No, not at all. Today's worker has a very different view of the world than his or her counterpart of the '90s.

6. No. In a time of dramatic change, experience can be a real drawback. It keeps us from dealing with new concepts from a fresh perspective.

7. Yes. Knowing what's going on reduces tension.

8. Yes, this helps to anticipate change — makes a company proactive rather than reactive.

9. Yes. Future-oriented companies are moving away from the traditional hierarchical structures.

10. No. This is a holdover from years back.

If you answered all these statements correctly, proceed immediately to the next chapter. Otherwise, read through Chapter 12 and learn more about a most difficult personal and organizational problem.

Chapter 13

Test What You Know About Technical Differences

What is different about managing technical people? Answer each question, then go to the end of the chapter to see how you did.

	Yes	No
1. Advances in technology allow managers to have more control over an employee's activities.	☐	☐
2. Managers need to control the kind and amount of information shared with employees.	☐	☐
3. Employees need to work in close proximity with each other to share information.	☐	☐
4. Managing employees at a distance is no different than when they are close to you.	☐	☐
5. The information that a business needs to operate changes as the technology changes.	☐	☐
6. Increases in technology require a manager to trust employees more, not less.	☐	☐
7. Allowing employees free access to the Internet affects productivity positively.	☐	☐
8. Letting them master the intricacies of the technology they work with can motivate employees.	☐	☐
9. The more interesting and engaging the work, the less supervision an employee needs.	☐	☐
10. Technology changes us as we become accustomed to it.	☐	☐

Chapter 13

Managing Technical People

Technology's Role in Change

Changes resulting from technology have always been with us. In a sense, the history of civilization is the history of technology. Civilizations move forward as various discoveries open up new options for how we relate to the environment. Control of fire, the wheel, and agriculture are all examples of early breakthroughs that changed humankind's relationship with the surrounding world forever.

Technology changes the way we look at the world; it changes the way we think about time and space. In earlier ages, time and space were inseparable. Moving anything through space took observable blocks of time. It took almost three months for Benjamin Franklin to bring the news to the French court that the United States was at war with England. The news was totally dependent upon the length of time it took a sailing ship to move through the space that separated the two continents. Time and space were tied tightly together.

Time was originally measured in seasons, the time unit of nomadic and agricultural societies. As civilizations developed, cultures began to think in months and weeks, then days, hours, minutes, and seconds — clock time. With the development of high-speed computer technology, the time unit has been reduced to almost nothing. The development of technology has been the process of separating time from space and shrinking time to smaller and smaller increments.

Managing in the Information Age

Today information technology is having a major impact on our lives. It continues the process of altering the way we look at space and time. Information technology is not new; it has been a major factor in the development of modern civilization since before the invention of the printing press. What makes technology so powerful today is its marriage to the computer. The computer has made more information available to more people than ever before in history. Nowhere is this truer than in the world of modern business.

Now, because of the availability of information at all levels in an organization, the role of the manager has changed. Previously, management positions could be defined by the level of access the manager had to important information, and how much he or she was authorized — or inclined — to share it. Today it is no longer possible to manage effectively by restricting the flow of information to employees. Workers no longer receive all their information from the hands of their immediate supervisors. Computer networking makes it possible to obtain information from many organizational sources. Information technology has reversed the information flow.

Information technology is also changing the way managers and workers are physically grouped. One of the reasons workers have been clustered together in the past has been the need for the close supervision of work. Today there are a number of situations where employees can theoretically be anywhere and still do their jobs. But what impact might this have on the manager's role? Most traditional management techniques assume that the manager and subordinate are somewhere near each other. The manager can observe the employee at work and is then able to take measures to ensure that all is working smoothly and well. Many of us can still remember the rooms filled with workers at desks, dominated by the manager's office with a window through which he or she could watch everyone.

Furthermore, working in close proximity also allowed quick and accurate passage of documents and memos of various kinds. As technology has progressed, starting with the typewriter, the telephone, the fax, and now the computer, the need for work-related proximity has steadily decreased. Messages and documents can now travel accurately around the world in a shorter time than it used to take to get them into the next room! But most workers still remain in offices and cubicles in large, impersonal buildings. This is largely because the kinds of management skills necessary to manage at a distance have not kept up with the technology available. The traditional management skill set does not include the option of employee self-management. Thus, a number of companies, having experimented with telecommuting, have brought these employees back into the office because of the lack of the proper skills for supervising them.

Managing at a distance requires some special skills, most of which are extensions of the techniques that you are learning in this book. But more importantly, it requires an attitude regarding the competence and honesty of the people reporting to you that is really at the core of what managing people is all about. As Douglas McGregor, an early management theorist, pointed out a number of years ago, it boils down to whether a manager believes that people are basically good or basically evil.[6] In McGregor's Theory X/Theory Y model, Theory X managers believe that employees are lazy, dislike responsibility, and prefer to be led. Theory Y managers believe that employees are responsible, motivated to work hard, and capable of self-direction. Given that the traditional management culture has not evolved very far toward employee self-direction, it is easy to understand why managing employees at a distance has become such a challenge.

Changes in Gathering Information

The information that a business needs to operate usually stays the same regardless of the kinds of technology used to access it. For example, a business always needs to have a prompt and accurate answer to questions like: "How much does the customer owe us?" and "How much do we owe to others?" There are many other critical questions, of course, regarding payroll, parts, distribution, and so on, but regardless of the technology

---

6. Douglas McGregor, *The Human Side of Enterprise,* Reprint edition, McGraw-Hill, Higher Education Series, 1985.

available to provide such information, the answers to these same questions have been critical since businesses were keeping track of their affairs by carving on flat rocks.

Although the information required to do business hasn't changed much, the technology to deliver it has. Not too long ago one of us entered into a somewhat complicated real estate transaction that required opening several escrows at the same time. All the transactions were accomplished smoothly and on time. It required, however, the extensive use of computers, faxes, and e-mail. It probably could not have been accomplished without such technology. Nonetheless, the information required by lenders, brokers, and escrow officers was virtually unchanged from what it was in the times when transactions were conducted without such advanced technology.

Technology has increased the amount of information that can be made available at low cost. It was always desirable to know as much about the customer as possible — information that could make it possible to predict buying habits, for example. But until the fast data-processing capabilities of computers became cheap and plentiful, such information was too costly and hard to retrieve to be of real value. Now the use of credit cards and the Internet allows organizations to collect and update thousands of bytes of data on every customer.

Technology has also decreased the amount of space necessary to store information. What used to take rooms filled with file cabinets can now be contained on a computer chip or a disk drive. Since buildings were designed to keep these stored documents close at hand for reference purposes, many thousands of square feet of dead space were built into the designs of buildings. Much of this storage is no longer necessary, since with computers linked together and providing a continuous flow of data, information is available in an instant. All this means that in the future there will be more information moving faster than ever before. Each employee will be able to process more information faster than their predecessors ever dreamed of. Thus, managers are going to need skills that are outside the bounds of what constitutes general management practice today. Employees will be scattered and, in order to work productively, will require a much more permissive and less hierarchical method of management. The key to this change in management style is trust.

As pointed out in previous chapters, trust grows through openness and honesty and is developed by interaction and teamwork. It happens when employees can be themselves, can be responsible to their organization, and can be acknowledged and rewarded for the ways they choose to combine the two.

Another Perspective on Employee Motivation

History indicates that information technology promotes freedom. It is no surprise that in a dictatorship, be it governmental or corporate, the means of disseminating information are under tight control. At first glance, it can appear that technology is controlling freedom. Companies are able to install software to monitor workplace behavior in ways unheard of until recently. But these controls are often the result of fear about the amount of freedom that is now available. The Internet has let the outside world come streaming into the workplace. If ways are developed to determine if an employee is surfing the Internet instead of working, it is because employees are taking advantage of the expanded horizons that the Internet offers. Perhaps the answer is to let employees organize their work in ways that will make it more interesting, instead of attempting to control it. Playing computer games and surfing the net may free up and rest workers' minds, actually increasing workers' productivity. Information technology changes the relationship between freedom and constraint in the workplace. Building trust is the key to making this change work for both employees and their organizations.

A New Mind-Set About Intelligence

Everyone has seen how captivated children are with computers. The computer engages large portions of their minds, perhaps even more than reading, some studies show. This engagement is pleasurable and exciting to them. There are too many synapses in today's young brains for children to numb out as their parents and grandparents did in office and assembly-line America. If constrained, they will resist. It is the teenagers and twenty-year-olds who hack into computer systems and invent computer viruses. The more opportunity employees have to master the intricacies of the technology related to their jobs, the more motivated they will become, and the more able they will be to operate without close supervision. They are going to master these intricacies anyway, so why not for the benefit of their organizations as well as themselves?

The human mind is capable of thinking at tremendous speeds. It can also process enormous amounts of data at these speeds. In most cases, the more the capacity of a worker's mind is utilized, the less day-to-day supervision he or she needs. Scientists, scholars, university professors, and engineers in research and development laboratories need practically no supervision at all, yet they produce at the highest levels. This is because they must operate closer to their full mental capacity than the average worker needs to.

The new generation of workers has been raised on digital information technology. We need to adapt traditional methods of management to reflect that fact. Information technology has brought the possibility of mental stimulation down through the organization to the most entry-level positions. It has also brought structure into these jobs because of the manner in which computer programs handle data. The constraints computer technology puts on the ways employees get things done allow managers to be more results-oriented and less concerned about the way workers go about their jobs. Under these conditions a supervisor becomes able to help employees develop their skills and broaden their horizons.

All this suggests that we may have to change our thinking about intelligence. Literacy and intelligence have long been seen as highly correlated in industrial societies. The very concept of the IQ test is based on that assumption, but recent discoveries in the area of emotional intelligence suggest this may not be the case.

On the one hand, literacy appears to be on the decline all over America. On the other hand, there is a lot less reason for children and adults to read and write well. The average American spends over seven and one-half hours a day watching television or surfing the Internet. That constitutes an extraordinary amount of information exposure, little of which requires reading and writing. If so much information is available without the need to read and write, there is little incentive to do so, especially among younger people. But the rest of us are affected, too. Take a look at your writing hand and see if you still have a writing callous on one of your fingers. Has it gotten smaller over the last few years? Most of us write so much less now that gripping a pen or pencil is no longer a constant activity. Many pens are sold now with a built-in cushion for the writer's comfort, a blessing if your writing callous has softened and shrunk!

Looking Toward the Future

There is no doubt that information technology will continue to influence future changes in managing people. Organizations are on the brink of massive transformation as a result of this phenomenon. However, there are many aspects of this process that we do not yet understand. As Marshal McLuhan said about technology, "First we shape our tools, and then our tools shape us." In other words, the more we engage with technology, the more we change in order to conform to its constraints. And computer technology can be quite rigid. The more advanced it is, the more procedures must be followed in order to obtain its benefits. On the other hand, unlike filing, typing, and assembly-line work, interaction with information technology seems to stimulate the intellect, not deaden it.

Interaction with today's information technology is producing an independent and intelligent workforce. Such potential can best be utilized in an organizational setting that is flat, flexible, and team focused. For the first time, Frederick Herzberg's insight that work itself motivates workers can be explored at almost every level of American business and industry. Employees no longer need to leave their minds at home when they report to work. Managers must be able to expand their skills to respond to this challenge.

What's Different About Technical Workers?

Most technical employees are more intelligent, creative, and independent than cubical workers in other positions. While their independence makes them less likely to be team members of their own volition, they understand that the difficult projects they undertake require a good deal of collaboration with others. The team-oriented manager can enhance their productivity and interest by being a team builder. (See chapters 2 and 3.) Similarly, full-fledged delegation is mandatory with creative people — they want to do things themselves. (See Chapter 6.) To be a successful manager of technical people it is essential to make the personal changes and apply the concepts that have been advocated throughout this book.

Additional Information

Books

Management: Leading People and Organizations in the 21st Century, Gary Dessler, Prentice-Hall Division, 2000. Shows how technology and e-business issues are affecting managers today.

Managing Technical People, Watts S. Humphrey, Addison-Wesley, 1996. Written for project leaders and managers. Delivers advice on how to best deal with talented, technically-minded people.

Managing Engineers and Technical Employees, Douglas M. Soat, Artech House, 1996. A former human resources executive characterizes technical employees as more intelligent, careful, creative, curious, introverted, and independent. He advises how to attract, motivate, and retain them.

People and Technology in the Workplace, National Academy of Engineering and Commission on Behavioral Science, National Academy Press, 1991. Case studies document successful transitions to new systems and procedures.

How to Interpret the Test for Chapter 13

Check your answers.

1. Yes, but at the cost of demotivating them.

2. Many may want to, but today it is next to impossible.

3. No. Computer technology makes it possible to share information over great distances.

4. No. Distance managing requires an emphasis on employee results as opposed to how and where they were obtained.

5. No. The basic information a business needs to function seems to remain the same.

6. Yes. Advances in technology require employees to work more independently.

7. Yes. Working with the Internet stimulates the mind and keeps employees more alert.

8. Yes. The more stimulated employees are by the challenges of their jobs, the more productive they are.

9. Yes. Employees avoid work when it is not interesting and thus need to be overseen more.

10. Yes. Each generation of technology requires different behaviors on the parts of those who use it.

Chapter 14

Test Your TQ – Transformational Quotient

Are you ready for the transformation? Last chance to check the boxes. The answers are at the end of this chapter.

	Yes	No
1. Intuition is as important as hard data in the decision-making process.	☐	☐
2. A person's belief system should not be open to question.	☐	☐
3. Reasonable risk-taking is important in all facets of life.	☐	☐
4. The power of our minds is relatively limited.	☐	☐
5. A shared corporate vision is valuable in moving an organization into new dimensions of excellence.	☐	☐
6. We can tap into other levels of consciousness, expanding our abilities in new ways.	☐	☐
7. Everyone has intuitive powers; we need only learn how to use them.	☐	☐
8. Spiritual issues belong in church.	☐	☐
9. In the management of people, everything should always make sense.	☐	☐
10. The ability to slip easily into a relaxed, altered state of consciousness is an important asset for an evolving manager.	☐	☐

Chapter 14

Transforming

> And now here is my secret,
> a very simple secret:
> It is only with the heart
> that one can see rightly;
> what is essential
> is invisible to the eye.
>
> Antoine de Saint-Exupery
> *The Little Prince*

The Paradigm Shift

For most of our lives as managers, we work at surviving, putting out fires, making short-term decisions. We need to satisfy executives, stockholders, partners, peers, or families. Sometimes we allow ourselves the small luxury of looking into the future through strategic planning. That's our reality.

We ask you to join us in exploring another reality or, more accurately, many other realities. These realities offer new ways of perceiving the world of work, ways that can substantially alter our lives for the better.

A growing perception in substantial segments of the scientific, academic, social science, government, and business communities suggests we are in the middle of a major paradigm shift. A paradigm is a framework of thought, a scheme for explaining and understanding certain aspects of reality. Our present paradigm is based on rational, logical, so-called "scientific" methods of understanding what our world is about.

A paradigm shift is a totally new way of thinking about old problems. It occurs when a great many new conceptual frameworks put pressure on old ones. An example of such a major shift is the Renaissance. It's easy to see the immense changes in historical perspective, but it's doubtful that many people sat around together in the fifteenth century saying to each other, "See, we're in the middle of the Renaissance." Talking about transformation from this earthbound perspective is presumptuous at best.

Still, the evidence of dramatic change is everywhere. As we saw earlier, studies show deep cultural changes. More people and institutions are grappling with questions about the meaning of their activities; they are concerned about the quality of life; they seek spiritual growth; they are reaching for higher potentials of human consciousness. The global terrorism threat and shifts in the ecological balance create a one-worldness that transcends all boundaries. Business organizations seem to react last to major change, so the current frenetic activity to improve how we handle people is an even more certain sign that we are in a paradigm shift.

What is the shape of this transformation? Perceiving a new level of consciousness while one is still anchored in the old is difficult, so you must begin by accepting the possibilities of an entirely new belief system. In the motion picture *The Empire Strikes Back*, Luke Skywalker's spaceship has become mired in a swamp. Yoda, wizard and mentor, helps Luke by calmly levitating the ship to dry land. "I don't believe it!" exclaims Luke in amazement. "That," observes Yoda, "is why you fail."

Intuition

The first step in transcending ordinary boundaries is discovering, accepting, and using intuition. In America, practically all of our training is in logical, linear thought-processing using the left hemisphere of the brain. We learn the importance of analysis, step-by-step procedures, and rational statements. A second way of knowing uses the right hemisphere. With the right side of the brain we dream, use metaphors, create new ideas. We see how parts go together to make up the whole, how things exist in space. Images rather than words are its tools.

You may laugh at this, but to get across the notion of intuition we have drawn on a scientific explanation of the functions of the brain — a linear way of describing the process that is sure to appeal to the rational mind.

When really being transformational, you do not need to add logic to what is another way of knowing. Intuition is simply intuition. All of us have experienced it. What's important is to accept it, trust it, and use it to put yourself in touch with the special knowledge that can be used to enhance your life.

The masculine culture of the Western world has devalued intuition. The message is that such ways are for poets, artists, and women. We believe that anything which cannot be perceived through the senses and judged rationally is not important. However, part of the transformation is the rediscovery of intuition. Top executives and keen managers are learning that their "gut feeling" may well be their highest power. Certainly, in people issues, intuition is more potent than logic.

Powers of the Mind

Reality is what we take to be true.

What we take to be true is what we believe.

What we believe is based upon our perceptions.

What we perceive depends on what we look for.

What we look for depends on what we think.

What we think depends on what we perceive.

What we perceive determines what we believe.

What we believe determines what we take to be true.

What we take to be true is our reality.[7]

An Olympic boxer sits quietly in a corner of the dressing room before his big fight. Deeply relaxed, eyes closed, he visualizes himself going into the ring at round one, performing flawlessly, watching and waiting for his opponent to leave an opening. Continuing his movie of the mind, he sees himself gaining strength and control in round two. In round three, his opponent drops his guard momentarily and our boxer sees himself moving in with the knockout punch.

He awakens from his mental exercise feeling relaxed and fit, walks into the ring and, just as visualized, knocks his opponent out in the third round.

---

7. Gary Zukav, *The Dancing Wu Li Masters* (New York: Bantam, 1979), p. 313.

In a San Francisco therapy group, cancer patients visualize their white blood cells as warriors with swords attacking and destroying cancer cells. After many weeks of this visualization exercise, some members of the group experience a remission of their symptoms.

In a research laboratory at Princeton University, student volunteers flip coins at random and learn to change the outcome by using mind control.

A group of executives goes through its regular problem-solving session, recording the results of its collective thinking. Then, for ten minutes, the executives meditate, noticing what surfaces in their minds about the problems they have been discussing. At the end of the meditation, they post the new ideas they have generated. To no one's amazement, they find many new solutions to their problems.

Dozens of books, hundreds of monographs, and thousands of experiments show the incredible power of the human mind. The ability to join minds across space and time is well known. How often have you found yourself thinking of exactly the same thing as someone else who is with you? Development of that ability leads to transformational possibilities in relationships. In the organization, it means that well-developed teams can transcend ordinary boundaries of communication and work together in an organic flow, linked by the extended use of their minds. This is not science fiction.

The Quantum Leap

For many people, a transformation comes about in one huge jump. Often the sudden change comes as the result of a deep trauma or a life crisis. Impending death, losing one's lifelong mate, losing the job held for many years — these and similar events have catapulted many people into a new way of viewing the world. Others go through the transformation as a result of some deep spiritual insight, sometimes connected with an orthodox religion. Often this insight results in the discovery of a spirituality of their own. There are many other ways of going through a transformation, but most seem to entail a sudden "splat" — a recognition that instantly everything has changed.

Reports of individual transformation have been surfacing everywhere for a number of years. They are so common that they have become an important consideration in the management of people. But beyond the individual, we are witnessing the beginning of the transformation of our organizations. Entire companies are restyling their view of who they are and their purpose and mission. Companies that excel seem to have a shared vision. Such visions come about through joined minds, one aspect of transformation.

The Transformational Organization

To transform, in the larger view, is to go beyond the known, to become comfortable with the unknown, to always be discovering. To transform is to create your own reality, not depending on others to point out the path, and to revel in your own uniqueness. Transforming is seeing 360 degrees at once, grasping the wholeness of what is, perceiving the universality in everything.

Transformation in a relationship is where two people are separate and yet simultaneously fold into each other. Transforming is dreaming, then becoming, the impossible dream.

Transformation, in the context of managing people, embodies many of the concepts advocated throughout the book. While these concepts are consistent with the culture already in place, they are also poised for a quantum leap. Taking these ideas just a step further produces organizations with totally new characteristics.

Jack Gibb, in *The Magic of Self-Regulation*,[8] describes the self-regulating organization. He says, "If I look at organizations and ask myself, 'How can I manage this enterprise?' I get answers that look something like the classic management textbooks. However, if I should ask such a question as 'How can I create an organization that will manage itself?' I am likely to come up with quite different answers." He goes on to describe transformational organizations as those that are able to operate without any traditional structure. These are their most critical characteristics:

- They are collaborative. In teams, they focus the energy of the organization on the job itself, on being creative.
- There is a flow, a harmony within the group, a synergy of movement.
- Everyone is discovering, questing, experimenting, excited about learning.
- Everyone owns the job, the team, the company, the mission. There is entrepreneurship at all levels.

---

8. Jack Gibb, "The Magic of Self-Regulation." Unpublished manuscript.

- There is super energy, artistry, trust, invention, breakthrough.
- Everyone has a deep sense of corporate mission — common goals, vision, perspective, wholeness.

Tom Peters emphasizes the importance of self-managed teams in the transformational organization: "The power of self-managing teams has been demonstrated in numerous settings. Why do they work? Quite simply, people in groups of ten to thirty can get to know one another well, can learn virtually everyone else's tasks, can be brought together with little fuss, and under enlightened leadership can readily achieve unit cohesion and esprit."[9]

Other characteristics of transformational organizations tie in with Gibb's notion of self-regulation:

- They place great emphasis on ethics and integrity.
- Commitment to excellence is collective. No one settles for less than the best. Everyone joins in the effort and shares in the psychic rewards of achievement.
- They foster and support individual growth within the team framework, while honoring individual differences.
- The organizations provide an atmosphere of attunement.
- Empowerment of others is an important part of their corporate code.
- The environment and the company's relationship with other systems are compelling concerns.
- They are committed to service.
- They are fun places to be.

For many people, the concept of individual and organizational transformation is beyond reality. But for others who have made the leap, that beyondness is their new reality.

The Transformational Manager

Managers taking their team or company into the beyondness of transformation — excellence, fulfillment, pure joy — are "imagineers." They have a vision or purpose outside the ordinary, outside the known. Those

---

9. Tom Peters, *Thriving on Chaos* (New York: Knopf, 1987), pp. 297–303.

who go with them on the journey find themselves being elevated to a higher level, until the teaming becomes an entity of such power that it transforms not only its own organizational environment, but all the systems it contacts.

Many such people of high purpose are now emerging in our society. Here's how you can recognize them.

- They are discoverers, constantly finding out new things about their own processes, about company processes. Wonder, excitement, and adventure are part of this focus. They don't resort to time-tested ways, forms, or structures. Firmly planted in the now, they are seeing into the new.

- They have a high sense of purpose and strong spiritual values. To them, spirituality is universality. They are members of the community of humankind.

- Intuition is a regular part of their lives. They use it naturally and easily. They trust their intuition; they have little need to rationalize it away. They keep in contact with their intuition by being relaxed, in touch with themselves, receptive.

- They value risk-taking in themselves and others.

- They do not look for teachers, gurus, or leaders. They find what they need within themselves and in their connection with alternative ways of knowing.

- They are collaborative. Teaming with others releases a group energy that is in itself transforming. They do not foster competition or engage in depersonalizing organizational politics.

- As co-creators of the corporate mission, they are dedicated to its high purpose. They focus on this mission, not on getting stuck in lesser goals such as power and image.

- They live comfortably with doubt, uncertainty, and ambiguity. Paradox is okay. Everything doesn't have to make sense.

- They see obstacles as challenges, everything as possible, jobs to do as easy. Whatever they are doing is fun. They convey this spirit to others.

- They practice becoming more conscious — using more of their innate powers — by shutting down the inner chatter to allow contact with other levels within themselves. Some meditate, others do varying styles of deep relaxation, but all of these activities exhibit a high purpose.

- Transformational managers trust their own inner processes, discovering who they are, becoming all they can be. Fear constrains. Trust frees.

- Transformational managers are entrepreneurs. They don't just go along with the system. They are constantly breaking out of the mold.

- Transformational managers think of themselves as mind-body-spirit — everything going at once.

Do you want to become a manager who can fulfill the needs of today and move easily into tomorrow? You can, if you want it badly enough. The key word is desire — a burning ambition to be all you were meant to be. The human potential is limitless, but we hold ourselves back with self-inflicted myopia.

If you are ready to move up, consider these ways of joining the ranks of transformational managers:

- Don't be afraid to explore yourself. Look for new facets, find hidden potential. See what parts of your life are not working and make plans to fix them. A transcendent person begins with the obvious — relationships, job, commitments.

- Get relaxed. Do deep relaxation daily. Being tense or under pressure is an absolute barrier to moving up. Learn to be calm.

- Line up a support system. Surround yourself with people who are headed in the same direction as you. Groups of people and organizations all over the country are committed to transformation.

- Believe! This is critical. What you believe creates your reality. If you believe you can go beyond, you will.

- Don't search for knowledge. Just continually prepare yourself. As an old Chinese saying states, "When the pupil is ready, the teacher will come."

- Don't substitute intuition for reason. Add it on. You need both.

- Development of an intuitive awareness involves suspension of judgment and evaluation. New knowledge needs empty space to enter.

- When you get a hunch, follow it all the way to the end.

- Allow the spiritual part of you to grow.

- Look at everything in new ways. Instead of saying, "This is the way we always did it," ask, "What are new ways we can look at it?"

- Let go of power. Be an empowerer of others. Empowerment is, in itself, a transformational force.

- Focus on excellence, artistry, and trust, never on fear and defense.

- Develop a passive, receptive state of mind that eliminates interference with the new knowledge available to you.

- Engage in the full range of health practices described in Chapter 9.

- Keep a journal of ideas — random thoughts that come to you during the day. Just the keeping is important, but reading it over now and then will give you surprising insights.

Management is much more than dealing with products, sales, or finances. The heart of management is working with people — and working well with people comes from the heart.

A Checklist for Developing Intuition

Intuition is something you can develop. It is a human ability that everyone possesses. By using and strengthening your intuitive powers, you can substantially expand your decision-making ability. Begin by running through this checklist of practices to help your intuition to come through. Then start doing the visualization exercises that follow; they can bring you amazing results.

- ☐ Incubate. Do nothing. Shift attention to another activity. Just let it happen. One famous inventor "sits for an answer." He goes into a dark, soundproof room, sits down, clears his mind and focuses on a single point until the idea he is seeking appears.

- ☐ Get rid of your cultural inhibitions. Track down any negative ideas you may have about intuition. List them and write down where you learned them. Neutralize negatives by finding reasons to believe. Use positive affirmations (mental repetitions) if necessary.

- ☐ Be in a state of readiness. Believe that the information coming to you is valuable. Be open to anything you receive.

- ☐ Quiet your mind. While your left brain is busy processing data, your right brain can't get through. Meditative practices are useful for maintaining an inner silence.

- ☐ Be relaxed. When tension is released, intuition can come into your awareness.

- ☐ Be honest with yourself. You can have clarity about incoming messages only if you face the truth. The busyness of pretending obscures vision.

☐ Trust is the core process. Trust yourself, trust others, and trust the experiences you are having. With high trust always comes low fear, further clearing the way for intuition.

☐ Pay attention every day. Purpose makes intuition happen.

☐ Build a support group. Have a few friends or an ongoing group where you can meet and share your intuitive experiences. Other people in the same process will help facilitate your growth.

Visualization

The most potent method for using intuitive powers in a purposeful way is visualization. By using a specific process, you can tap into your intuition. The beginning of any visualization process is to go into a deeply relaxed state. Quiet your mind. You can use a method of your own or you can use the deep relaxation described at the end of Chapter 9.

When you are fully relaxed, try some of these visualizations:

• When you have a problem you wish to solve, visualize yourself in the Himalaya Mountains. See yourself climbing a mountain, going way up to a cave. Enter the cave where sits a wise guru. Tell the guru about your problem and listen as he gives you a solution. This is an excellent way to reach information below your level of consciousness.

• Visualize a chalkboard. Keep focused on the chalkboard until a message appears.

• For looking into the future, visualize a video player inside your head. See a screen out front. Imagine that the film is your life story. Start the tape at your childhood and let it play rapidly through the years. When it gets to the present do not stop it, but allow it to play on into the future. Stop the film at any point in time and watch how your life unfolds.

• To check out how you are making choices in your life, do a visualization review of the past twenty-four hours. What choices did you make? Did you make them using intuition? Were the choices satisfactory? What other choices did you have?

• For getting to understand someone better, visualize yourself in your favorite place of relaxation. Invite the other person to join you. Strike up a conversation. Notice everything you can about the other person. Ask as many questions as you need to. When you are done, visualize a perfect parting. The next time you are with this person, notice how you feel and act.

- For another way of getting at a problem, write down whatever is troubling you. Put it in the form of a question. Then go into relaxation. Imagine yourself on the shore of a calm lake. A small boat waits there. Get into the boat, raise the sail, and head off toward an island in the distance. On the shore of the island notice a person. As you get closer, see if you recognize who it is. Just notice. Silently, pull up onto the shore. The person hands you a package. You accept in silence, turn, get into the boat and set sail for the mainland. Back on the mainland, open your package and examine the contents. Open your eyes and bring your awareness back to the present.

What did the gift signify for you? If nothing connects for you at the moment, just let it simmer. Important insights may come to you at a later time.

Additional Information

Books

Is It Always Right to be Right?, Warren Schmidt and B.J. Hateley, Amacom, 2001. An illustrated tale of transforming workplace conflict into creativity and collaboration. Tips on handling conflict, too.

The New Pioneers: Men and Women Who Are Transforming the Workplace and Marketplace, Thomas Petzinger, Jr., Touchstone Books, 2000. A Wall Street Journal columnist examines how employees are getting the leeway to manage themselves and are in the forefront of an economic seachange.

Change the World, Robert E. Quinn, Jossey-Bass, 2000. Examples from Jesus, Ghandi, and Martin Luther King advise that to become a change agent you must first change yourself.

Awakening Corporate Soul: Four Paths to Unleash the Power of People at Work, Eric Klein and John B. Izzo, Fairwinds Press, 1998. A yogi and a minister, who are also business consultants, mix Eastern and Western ideas to suggest new ways to develop a more motivated and committed workforce.

The Memory Triggering Book, Robert M. Wendlinger, Proust Press, 1995. Access to your treasured memories can enhance your understanding of who you are and where you are going.

The Leadership Challenge, James Kouzes and Barry Posner, Jossey-Bass, 1995. Describes what's at the heart of transforming leadership.

Wherever You Go There You Are, Jon Kabat-Zinn, Hyperion, 1994. Mindful meditations, artful simplicity, deep insights.

Intuition Workbook, Marcia Emery, Prentice-Hall, 1994. Exercises for enhancing intuitive abilities.

A Path With Heart, Jack Kornfield, Bantam Books, 1993. A guide through the perils and promises of spiritual life.

Intuition in Organizations, Weston H. Agor, editor, Sage Publications, 1989. A collection of articles on business applications of intuition.

Global Mind Change, Willis Harman, Knowledge Systems, Inc., 1988. A wonderfully concise and profoundly hopeful guide to the great transformation now occurring on our planet.

The Intuitive Manager, Roy Rowan, Little Brown and Company, 1986. The revelations of top CEOs give new credence to the importance of intuition in the executive suite.

Transforming Leadership, John D. Adams, editor, Miles River Press, 1986. A series of articles on the role and thinking of leaders faced with complex and turbulent environments.

How to Interpret the Test for Chapter 14

Future-oriented managers would answer "Yes" to numbers 1, 3, 5, 6, 7, and 10.

Future-oriented managers would answer "No" to number 2.

> They are constantly questioning their values as they receive new information and ideas.

The answer to number 4 is "No."

> We probably use about twenty percent of the power of our minds. Developing the ability to expand the mind is a prime challenge to today's leaders.

Most transformational managers would answer "No" to number 8.

> They understand that spirituality has a connotation that is not necessarily a part of organized religion. To them, it is the experience of something beyond their own boundaries. In pragmatic terms, it is living a life that embodies values such as integrity, love, empowerment of others, communicating fully — many of the concepts that have been advocated throughout this book.

The answer to number 9 is "No."

> Transformational managers learn to live comfortably with ambiguity, uncertainty, and paradox.

Index